Compete with Deceit

Break Through the Enemy's Lies and Embrace God's Truth That Sets You Free

By LAURA WOROSHER

ethos
collective

COMPETE WITH DECEIT © 2025 by Laura Worosher. All rights reserved.

Printed in the United States of America

Published by Igniting Souls
PO Box 43, Powell, OH 43065
IgnitingSouls.com

This book contains material protected under international and federal copyright laws and treaties. Any unauthorized reprint or use of this material is prohibited. No part of this book may be reproduced or transmitted in any form or by any means, electronic or mechanical, including photocopying, recording, or by any information storage and retrieval system, without express written permission from the author.

LCCN: 2025902127
Paperback ISBN: 978-1-63680-468-2

Available in paperback

Scripture quotations, unless otherwise indicated, are taken from the Holy Bible, New International Version®, NIV®. Copyright © 1973, 1978, 1984 by Biblica, Inc.™ Used by permission of Zondervan. All rights reserved worldwide.

Scripture quotations marked (ESV) are from The ESV® Bible (The Holy Bible, English Standard Version®), © 2001 by Crossway, a publishing ministry of Good News Publishers. Used by permission. All rights reserved."

Scripture marked (NKJV) taken from the New King James Version®. Copyright © 1982 by Thomas Nelson. Used by permission. All rights reserved.

Any Internet addresses (websites, blogs, etc.) and telephone numbers printed in this book are offered as a resource. They are not intended in any way to be or imply an endorsement by Igniting Souls, nor does Igniting Souls vouch for the content of these sites and numbers for the life of this book.

Some names and identifying details may have been changed to protect the privacy of individuals.

The superscript symbol ^{IP} listed throughout this book is known as the unique certification mark created and owned by Instant IP™. Its use signifies that the corresponding expression (words, phrases, chart, graph, etc.) has been protected by Instant IP™ via smart contract. Instant IP™ is designed with the patented smart contract solution (US Patent: 11,928,748) which creates an immutable time-stamped first layer and fast layer identifying the moment in time an idea is filed on the blockchain. This solution can be used in defending intellectual property protection. Infringing upon the respective intellectual property, i.e., ^{IP}, is subject to and punishable in a court of law.

Other Books by Laura Worosher

Blind to Hope: See Beyond Your Darkness and Walk into God's New Vision for Your Life

Dedication

To my Lord and Savior, Jesus Christ, my Elohim Shomri: All glory to you for winning the war, and graciously, mercifully, strengthening your followers as we stand against the schemes of the devil. May I never lose sight of my weakness and your omnipotence.

To Tyler, my husband and battle buddy: We have fought side by side for 13 years now, and there's no person I'd rather stand back to back with against everything that life and the evil spiritual forces in the heavens throws at us. Thank you for having my back.

To Tristan, Tessa, and Lincoln, my precious children: You are already such strong warriors. I pray for strength, wisdom, and humility for each of you every day. Know that even when the lies of Satan seem overpowering, God is always stronger. My greatest joy as a mom is knowing that His Spirit lives inside you.

To the other battle-weary, scarred, wounded, followers of Christ and my heroes of the faith who have taught me what it looks like to fight with honor, to learn from my defeat and to always remember that no victory is achieved alone, I salute you. Mom and Dad, I'm thinking specifically of you here. I could not be more proud of my legacy of prayer warriors and examples of a God-honoring life.

Table of Contents

Introduction xi
Week 1: "You're Not Good Enough" 1
Week 2: "God Can't Forgive You for That" 11
Week 3: "God Doesn't Care About You or Your Struggles" 23
Week 4: "Your Worth Is Based on Your Performance or Appearance" 40
Week 5: "God Isn't Fair" 51
Week 6: "Your Past Defines You" 63
Week 7: "You Can Do This On Your Own" 78
Week 8: "Following God Is too Hard and not Worth It" . . 88
Week 9: "You Need _____ to Have Peace" 102
Week 10: "You'll Never Change" 114
Closing Comments 125
Endnotes 127
About the Author 129

Introduction

Have you ever told a lie? Some lies are big, like the ones I told my parents when I was a teenager about being at a friend's house when I was really out with my boyfriend. Some lies are smaller, like when I was a few minutes late to work or a lunch meeting and blamed it on the traffic instead of on the extra ten minutes I took to get ready.

If you can't relate to telling a big lie, you may be able to remember something smaller. Maybe you forgot to pay a bill or send an email or a birthday card, and you said something like, "It must have gotten lost or not come through yet."

Some lies don't get spoken out loud but are rather lies we tell ourselves. These sound a lot like, "It wasn't my fault," "That was out of my control," or "I couldn't have done anything to help anyway." In some cases, these thoughts may be true, but in others, they are a deceptive way to protect our pride and keep us from feeling guilty about a situation.

The thing about lies is they can start small but have a way of growing bigger. You tell a "small" lie to explain a situation, but upon further questioning, you have to continue to tell bigger and bigger lies to protect the one you told in the first place.

The other thing about lies is the more you tell them, the more comfortable you get with them. If you had asked me when I was younger if I would ever cheat on my spouse, I would have told you never in a million years. I never dreamed I would lie to my husband about where I was and who I was with because I was cheating on him.

How did I get there? I did not jump straight from faithful wife to cheating liar. When I was ten years old, a boy in my fifth-grade class had a crush on me. He would write me love letters. These letters were not graphic in any way but were still a bit too mature for a ten-year-old to be writing or receiving. I figured my parents wouldn't approve, so I hid the letters. Things done in secret have a way of coming out eventually, and my parents found the letters. I told them I would cut off my communication with the boy and stop the letters. But I liked the letters. They made me feel special. Wanted. So I didn't stop them. I just did a better job of hiding them.

I got better at lying. Remember the lie I told my parents about being out with a friend when I was really with my boyfriend? That started when I was fifteen. When I went to college at eighteen, I had a boyfriend back home. As typically happens when you go to college, I met a bunch of other guys. I went out on dates with quite a few of them and didn't tell my boyfriend. It wasn't until I had an official boyfriend at college that I broke up with my boyfriend from home. Even then, I blamed the breakup on the long-distance relationship rather than on meeting someone new.

I didn't stop there. I cheated on that boyfriend with several other guys. I used to tell myself I would stop lying and cheating when I eventually got engaged. Then I got engaged, but

Introduction

that didn't stop it. "It's just because I'm not married. I will stop cheating once I get married," I convinced myself.

I was actually surprised the first time I cheated on my husband. I should not have been. I should have seen it coming. I should have looked back on my track record of thirteen years of lying about men and relationships and realized I had become comfortable with lying. I was a liar. I lied to others and to myself as easily as I took a breath. Sometimes I would forget what was the lie and what was the truth. I was a mess.

Not a small mess, but a big, terrible mess. I hurt so badly on the inside from all the lies I had told, jumping from one shallow, meaningless fling to the next. I felt like I was rotting away and parts of me were already dead. It wasn't that I enjoyed lying. I hated it. I wanted to stop. I tried to stop. I confessed my sin over and over again and thought that if I just tried a little harder or prayed a little more, I could solve my lying problem. The mess just got worse.

Do you know who wasn't a mess? Who was enjoying my wreck of a life and all the lies I had told to get there? Satan. He was winning, and he knew it. In John 8:44, the Bible calls Satan "the father of lies" for good reason. Genesis 3:4 records the first lie told on earth. It comes in an encounter between Satan and the first woman, Eve: "You will not certainly die." His lies jump-started humankind down the path of evil and allowed the curse of sin to enter the world. Even before that, his lies to himself that he was worthy to be higher than God started the spiritual battle between good and evil. The Bible records this account in Isaiah 14.

If you read the Genesis 3 account of Satan's lies to Eve, you'll notice that they are not unbelievable. That's exactly what

Satan intended. He mixed his lies with just enough of the truth to cause Eve to doubt what God had really said. Satan still uses this tactic today. He whispers lies in our ears in much the same way he did to Eve. They don't always sound big or bad enough to cause hurt and destruction. But they always do. Even if it doesn't happen right away, one small lie can lead to unimaginable misery.

So, here we are. We know Satan is bombarding us with lies. What do we do? How do we respond? As a Christian, I have always considered myself to be on the defensive. I think of Bible verses like James 4:7, "**Resist** the devil, and he will flee from you." I think of the passage in Ephesians 6:10-17 about the armor of God:

> "[10] Finally, be strong in the Lord and in his mighty power. [11] Put on the full armor of God, so that you can **take your stand** against the devil's schemes. [12] For our struggle is not against flesh and blood, but against the rulers, against the authorities, against the powers of this dark world and against the spiritual forces of evil in the heavenly realms. [13] Therefore put on the full armor of God, so that when the day of evil comes, you may be able to **stand your ground,** and after you have done everything, to **stand.** [14] **Stand firm then,** with the belt of truth buckled around your waist, with the breastplate of righteousness in place, [15] and with your feet fitted with the readiness that comes from the gospel of peace. [16] In addition to all this, take up the shield of faith, with which you can extinguish all the flaming arrows of the evil one. [17] Take the helmet of salvation and the sword of the Spirit, which is the word of God." (emphasis added)

Introduction

Did you hear that? "Resist," "Take your stand," "Stand your ground," "Stand," "Stand firm then," these are all positions of defense. If you have heard a sermon on these verses before, you may recall this, but all the pieces of armor mentioned here are defensive weapons, except for one: The Sword of the Spirit. The belt, the breastplate, the sandals, the shield, and the helmet are all for protection and defense.

In addition, nowhere in Scripture is Jesus described as physically violent. When provoked, attacked, mobbed, tortured, and murdered, He never fought back.

When Satan came into the wilderness to tempt Jesus, Jesus didn't charge at Satan in a rage or make threats, as recorded in Matthew 4:1-11. He didn't call down an army of angels and give a battle cry. He didn't even seem to get riled up. He was calm, ready, and prepared. When He did go on the offensive and use the Scriptures—the sword of the spirit—it was not in an overly aggressive, vengeful way. It was steady, deliberate, and cut straight to the heart of what Satan was trying to accomplish in the wilderness that day.

Then there is Matthew 16:18, which reads, "And I tell you, you are Peter, and on this rock I will build my church, and the gates of hell shall not prevail against it" (ESV). Some have said this passage indicates that Christians will be storming the gates of hell. Further study, however, shows this is yet another description of biblical defense.

The Hebrew word used in that verse for "gates of hell" is *pulai hadou*, which is often translated as "realm of the dead" and refers to Hades.[1] That same term is also used in Job 38:17, "Have the gates of death been shown to you?" and in Isaiah

38:10, "I said, 'In the prime of my life must I go through the gates of death and be robbed of the rest of my years?'"

Both passages refer to the grave or the unseen place of the dead. It is also interesting to note that gates in Biblical times were places where councils and government met—places of strength and fortification. With that in mind, I understand the passage in Matthew 16:18 to mean the power and rule of Satan and the dead will not overcome the Church.

This is an incredible message of hope and strength! Yet, if our primary position as the Church and believers is one of defense, how will we be victorious over sin and Satan? Who is on the offense? One word. One name. The name that is above every name. Jesus.

He already defeated Satan when He burst from the grave, conquering death once and for all. The Bible says in Revelation 1:17-18, "When I saw him, I fell at his feet as though dead. Then he placed his right hand on me and said: 'Do not be afraid. I am the First and the Last. I am the Living One; I was dead, and now look, I am alive for ever and ever! And I hold the keys of death and Hades.'"

Acts 2:24 says, "But God raised him from the dead, freeing him from the agony of death, because it was impossible for death to keep its hold on him." He is our champion. He is the rock on which we stand. He and He alone is our hope for victory. Praise the Lord for the bloody cross and the empty tomb, and our savior Jesus who was willing to endure it all because of His love for you and me. Amen!

I finally came to realize I didn't have a lying problem. I had a heart problem. I believed in Jesus and had asked Him into my

Introduction

heart when I was younger, but I was still sitting in the driver's seat of my life. I thought I was strong enough to defeat sin and Satan on my own. I was fighting, but I was doing it without the armor of God and most definitely without acknowledging my greatest weapon was the Word of God.

I was lying because I was chasing men in a vain attempt to feel loved. Although I may have accepted Jesus as my savior, I hadn't accepted how much He loved me, how much I mattered to Him, and that His love was the only love that really mattered. I thought I needed the love of Jesus AND the love of others. I was a liar because I was believing the lie of Satan that Jesus's love was only part of the love I needed to feel complete.

Throughout the course of my life, I have fallen prey to many, many, many of Satan's lies. He is good at telling them and I am vulnerable to believing them. He speaks them to me every day. The closer I am to Jesus and the more of the Bible I memorize, the quicker I can identify and avoid or defeat the lies.

While not exhaustive by any means, this Bible study is designed to help arm you with specific Bible verses to help when you feel Satan whispering his lies to you. It can also help you identify some of the more common lies of Satan. Once you have identified them, it is easier to cry out to the Lord for help and use the Sword of the Spirit to defeat the lies. It is also easier to angle the deflector shields on your armor of God if you know your weak spots where Satan is most likely to pinpoint an attack.

Friend, let me remind you we are on the defensive here. None of us can defeat Satan or his lies on our own. First and foremost, we need to rely on the strength of our Champion, our Savior, and the already-crowned victor: the Lord Jesus Christ. With that in mind, let's gird our loins and prepare to compete with deceit!

The things we will be wrestling with in this study are not easy or light. I recommend only answering four or five questions each day. This will allow you time to ponder the questions and your responses and to meditate on the truths of scripture as you go along. If even that feels like a lot, please go at your own speed. The Lord's timing is perfect, and only you know the pace at which He is asking you to walk. Know that He has not asked you to walk this journey alone, and please feel free to reach out to me through my website if I can be of help.

··· Week 1 ···

The Lie: "You're Not Good Enough"

HOW MANY TIMES has that thought popped into your mind? I can count about ten in the last two hours. When I tossed some granola bars and apple juice to the kids and called it breakfast, forgot to tell my husband where I was going as I dashed out of the house because I was late, and skipped reading my Bible, I think, "I'm not a good enough mom, wife, or Christ-follower."

This list is not exhaustive, but I get exhausted thinking about all the areas where I don't measure up. Can you relate?

What are some of the areas where you feel you don't measure up?

_____
_____
_____
_____

You are not alone here. Everyone has areas like this, which is part of what makes this lie so effective. Let's go deeper into why these thoughts can be so pervasive.

Why the lie works:

Like most other lies from Satan, this one works because it's partially true. I'm not good enough. I should have made the kids a healthier breakfast, communicated with my husband, and read my Bible. I should witness with words more often, help more people without being asked, and not secretly want to spend the winter months sitting on a beach in Aruba all by myself. When I know I'm not good enough, I start to feel inadequate.

Thoughts about inadequacy typically originate from some sort of comparison, failure, or expectation. For example, in all of the above scenarios, I'm comparing myself to the construct in my mind of what a good mom, wife, or Christian is. I'm thinking about what others' expectations are for me in these areas. I'm thinking about all the ways I know I have fallen short in these roles.

The lie of "you're not good enough" works on us because somewhere deep inside, we are still trying to earn approval, respect, and love. We all yearn to have meaning and significance in our lives, which is not a bad thing, but becomes harmful when we seek validation from others or from our accomplishments.

Why this is a lie:

The truth is, while we are not good enough, Jesus is. More than good enough, He was perfect. Through his substitutionary atoning death on the cross, his perfection is credited to my account. He says that I am good enough. Not because I am the best mom, wife, friend, sister, employee, or even because I'm a decent human. Left to myself, I am none of those things. He says I am good enough because He is good enough, and He is living in me.

The other truth is that no one gets it right all the time. Most of us have tossed pre-packaged crap at our kids when we're running late in the morning at least once. Or we've gotten caught up in life and forgotten to text our spouses a word of encouragement. Or skipped a day of Bible reading. I am a chief offender in these areas.

The consequences of believing the lie:

"You're not good enough" is a lie from Satan designed to undermine our self-worth and God's unconditional love. If "you're not good enough" at something, will you get excited about improving in that area? Probably not. You will likely feel like me when I am caught in this lie and want to stop putting effort into that area altogether.

For example, when my kids have a rough day with homeschooling and there are meltdowns over math fractions and long division, my instinct is to give up. I think, "I'm not a good enough teacher. Maybe they would be better off going to school." I'm not excited about doing school again the next day.

If I continue to believe the lie that I am not good enough as a homeschool mom, I will suffer and my kids will suffer. My insecurity and doubt that comes from believing this lie will inhibit my ministry to my children. This is exactly what Satan wants. If he can disrupt my ministry in my home, it is a short hop to raising kids who lack passion for following Christ.

The truth and God's view of our worth:

- **Isaiah 41:10 – God thinks we are worth His help.** "So do not fear, for I am with you; do not be dismayed, for I am your God. I will strengthen you and help you; I will uphold you with my righteous right hand."

    Why does the Lord tell us not to fear?

    _____
    _____
    _____
    _____

    What does the Lord say He will do for us?

    _____
    _____
    _____
    _____

What are some things you need to ask God for help with?

_____
_____
_____
_____

- **Genesis 1:27 – He created us in His image.** *"So God created mankind in his own image, in the image of God he created them; male and female he created them."*

  What about being created in the image of God communicates value to you?

  _____
  _____
  _____
  _____

- **Isaiah 43:4 – We are precious in His sight.** *"Since you are precious and honored in my sight, and because I love you, I will give people in exchange for you, nations in exchange for your life."*

  What does God see when He looks at you if you are in Christ?

  _____
  _____
  _____
  _____

How do the things that God is willing to exchange for you communicate your worth to Him?

- **Ephesians 2:10 – He created us with purpose.** *"For we are God's handiwork, created in Christ Jesus to do good works, which God prepared in advance for us to do."*

  What does this verse say we are?

  How does knowing you were created intentionally by God for a specific purpose help you know you are valuable to Him?

- **Romans 8:37 – We are more than conquerors through Christ.** *"No, in all these things we are more than conquerors through Him who loved us."*

"You're Not Good Enough"

Not only are we valuable, but what else does God say we are in this verse?

_____
_____
_____
_____

- **John 15:16 – He chose and appointed us.** *"You did not choose me, but I chose you and appointed you so that you might go and bear fruit—fruit that will last…"*

    What two things did the Lord do in regards to you according to this verse?

    _____
    _____
    _____
    _____

    What do you think it means to be chosen? Think about a time you were picked for a role in the school play, or for a position on a team, or asked to be someone's girlfriend.

    _____
    _____
    _____
    _____

What do you think it means to be appointed? Think about a time when you were given a specific task to complete or a project to do.

_____
_____
_____
_____

You have been "chosen" and "appointed" by God. What kind of response do you have when you read that?

_____
_____
_____
_____

God's love is not based on our performance. Can I get an "AMEN!" Rather, it is based on His unconditional love and acceptance of us as His children. When we refuse to be blind to hope, but instead see ourselves through God's lens, He gives us a sense of peace, purpose and confidence.

Breaking free from the lie:

Here are some steps you can take to break free from this lie:

- **Replace it with affirmations of truth, such as, "I am fearfully and wonderfully made" (Psalm 139:14).**

  Write out five affirmations of truth from Scripture you can memorize to help you when you hear Satan start to whisper the lie that "you are not good enough."

"You're Not Good Enough"

_____
_____
_____
_____
_____

- **Cultivate gratitude**

    Write out five things you are grateful for right now:

    _____
    _____
    _____
    _____
    _____

- **Focus on your strengths**

    What are three areas where you feel God has gifted you?

    _____
    _____
    _____

- **Accept imperfections**

    What are three areas where you feel most tempted to believe the lie that "you are not good enough"?

    _____
    _____
    _____

- **Surround yourself with people who uplift, encourage, and remind you of your value. Sharing struggles with trusted friends, family, or a faith-based community can bring healing and help to dismantle this lie.**

Name three people you can talk to when you need encouragement to overcome this lie:

_____
_____
_____

Encouragement from community:

Everyone has a unique purpose and value that cannot be diminished by past mistakes or perceived inadequacies. The more we can speak into each other's lives with God's truth about each other, the more those truths will replace the lie that "you are not good enough" with the reality of our worth in Him.

··· Week 2 ···

The Lie: "God Can't Forgive You for That"

FOR WHAT? I used to think that I hadn't done anything really "bad." Sure, I had talked back to my parents, been jealous of my best friend's boyfriend, and told little white lies about why I was late to work, but those weren't a big deal. Everyone does those things.

Then they hit me. My teenage years. And my twenties. Before I knew it, I had racked up a list of "bad" sins a mile long. I had told huge, catastrophic lies (ask me about the time I was kicked out of Canada), cheated on boyfriends, driven drunk, and stolen money from friends, among other things. Somewhere along the way, I stopped reading my Bible and going to church. I felt too much shame for my "big" sins.

One of the most crippling lies we can believe is, *"God can't forgive me for that."* Although I know God will technically forgive me for my sins, it's hard to believe that He truly doesn't hold them against me. He forgives, but how can He forget?

How can He forget the lies I have told, the times I have cheated, the times I have lashed out in anger, the times I have wished my life looked different, the times I have chosen my way, my will, my desires over His? Because I will never fully forget the times people have hurt me, even when I have "forgiven" them. I still tend to feel that when God looks at me, all He sees is my sin. My huge, smelly, heaping mountain of sin.

This falsehood thrives in shame and isolation, convincing us we've gone too far for God's grace. When I am alone, it is so easy to recall past sins and feel unworthy. This lie of Satan works because it is true, all except for one word: CAN'T. God CAN forgive us, and He DOES forgive us. But in my heart, I know that He SHOULDN'T forgive me. I don't deserve it.

The truth is God's forgiveness is not limited by the depth of our mistakes—it's defined by the infinite depth of His love and mercy. The more I get involved in community and become vulnerable with others, the more I realize this shame is a common thread and God has forgiven each of His children for "big" and "little" sins. Sharing stories of His forgiveness with others is just one way to start healing and forgiving yourself. Here are other ways to overcome this destructive lie and step into the freedom of His forgiveness.

1. Recognize the Source of the Lie

This belief doesn't originate from God. Scripture clearly shows God desires to forgive and restore, not condemn. John

"God Can't Forgive You for That"

3:16 says, "For God so loved the world that he gave his one and only Son, that whoever believes in him shall not perish but have eternal life." It doesn't say, "Whoever believes in him and is good enough." All you need to do is believe. He will take care of the rest.

If you are a believer in Christ and have given your life to Him, take a moment to briefly write out your testimony:

_____
_____
_____
_____
_____
_____
_____

The very next verse, John 3:17, is one of my favorites in the whole Bible: "For God did not send his Son into the world to condemn the world, but to save the world through him."

Why did God send His Son into the world according to John 3:17?

_____
_____
_____
_____

Oh, how I deserve to be condemned. I deserve death. Yet for those who believe in Him, God is not up in heaven keeping track of our sins and waiting to punish us for them. To say it's a relief is the understatement of the century.

How does it make you feel to think that God's desire is to save you, not to condemn you?

_____
_____
_____
_____

Unfortunately, Satan doesn't want us to remember the truth of John 3:17. The enemy thrives on lies that distort our view of God and ourselves. His aim is to keep us bound in shame, unable to approach God for the forgiveness freely offered through Jesus Christ, as we mentioned previously when we talked about who Satan really is according to the Bible (John 8:44). Identifying this as a spiritual attack helps us resist it with truth.

The irony is that God has already forgiven us, and there is never a need to feel shame. Guilt, yes. Conviction, absolutely. This is another reason why this lie of Satan works. When we sin against God, we feel guilty. We can trace the feeling all the way back to Adam and Eve in the Garden of Eden. Sin always comes with a sense of guilt and conviction. That is healthy. It is the shame piece that is wrong.

While Adam and Eve hid from God in their shame, He was actively seeking them out, according to Genesis 3:8-9: "Then the man and his wife heard the sound of the Lord God as he was walking in the garden in the cool of the day, and they hid from the Lord God among the trees of the garden. But the Lord God called to the man, 'Where are you?'" He was not seeking them out to yell at or shame them, but to provide covering for them and give them His promise of redemption.

Hiding and running from God out of a sense of shame looks way different from running to God when we feel guilty and asking for forgiveness. Are you running away because you are caught in the lie that "God can't forgive you for that"? Or are you running to Him because you know He has already forgiven you, and confessing your sin is the only way to remove the feeling of guilt for breaking His heart?

2. Anchor Yourself in God's Word

The Bible is filled with evidence of God's abundant forgiveness. God knows how easy it is for us to feel shame and that we need constant reminders, so He filled Scripture with verses on forgiveness.

- **"If we confess our sins, He is faithful and just to forgive us our sins and to cleanse us from all unrighteousness" (1 John 1:9, ESV).**

    According to this verse, what is the only thing we have to do in order to receive forgiveness and cleansing?

    _____
    _____
    _____
    _____

- **"Though your sins are like scarlet, they shall be as white as snow" (Isaiah 1:18).**

    Did you catch that? How many stains of your sin will be left after Jesus cleanses you from them?

    _____

- "As far as the east is from the west, so far has He removed our transgressions from us" (Psalm 103:12).

    How far has He removed our transgressions? (Hint: the east and west never touch!)

    _____
    _____
    _____

    Because there isn't an east or west pole, there is no such thing as a starting point when traveling in that direction. You can't start at West. You could potentially start at the North Pole and travel south, and at some point you would stop traveling south and start traveling north again. Not so with the east and west. You could start traveling west, and continue to travel west for the rest of your life without reaching the east.

These promises aren't conditional upon the severity of our sins but are based on God's character and the finished work of Christ on the cross.

One of my favorite Bible passages is about the prodigal son in Luke 15:11-32. I love how it demonstrates God's forgiveness for both the son who blatantly hurt the father and chose to go his own way, as well as for the son who was stuck in pride and thought he didn't need the father. I am both those sons on a daily basis. God forgives me every day for my sins of pride and of loving the world too much.

"God Can't Forgive You for That"

Read Luke 15:11-32. Which son do you identify with more often?

How is the forgiveness of the father in this passage an example of how the Lord as our Father forgives us, His children?

---

3. Look to Jesus, Not Your Sin

Believing God can't forgive us often stems from focusing too much on the size of our sin rather than the size of our Savior. The cross is a vivid reminder that Jesus already paid the price for *all* sin, including the ones you're ashamed of. When Jesus declared, "It is finished" (John 19:30), He meant it. Nothing you've done is beyond the scope of His sacrifice. Not yelling at your kids. Not cheating on your spouse. Not lying on your taxes. Not being anxious about the future. Not anything.

What are some sins you tend to think of as being "big" or "unforgivable" in your life?

---

4. Break the Cycle of Shame

Shame tells us we must hide from God, but confession brings freedom. When we acknowledge our sin before God, we're not informing Him of something He doesn't already know. We're accepting His invitation to experience healing and restoration.

Shame also tells us we must hide from each other. If people knew who we really were or what we had done in the privacy of our own home or office or car, we would lose all our friends. The truth is we all have shameful stories of sin—all of us.

James 5:16 encourages us to confess to one another as well, so we can pray and find support in trusted community. Sharing our stories of God's victory over our past sins or those we are currently struggling with can provide the confidence we need to overcome the lie that "God can't forgive you for that."

List five people you can confess your sins to and lean on for accountability:

_____
_____
_____
_____
_____

5. Replace Lies with Truth

Combating this lie requires actively replacing it with God's truth. Whenever the thought, *"God can't forgive me for that,"* arises, counter it with Scripture:

- "There is now no condemnation for those who are in Christ Jesus" (Romans 8:1).

  How much condemnation is there for you as a believer? Write the answer several times:

  _____
  _____
  _____
  _____

- "Where sin increased, grace increased all the more" (Romans 5:20).

  There is no such thing as "small" sin, or "small" grace. Even one sin is enough to separate us from the holy God for all eternity. Grace is a costly gift that required the blood of a sinless savior. Rest assured, God's grace is big enough, encompassing enough, and surpassing enough to cover even our "biggest" of sins.

  List three specific ways you have witnessed the grace of God covering the sins in your life:

  _____
  _____
  _____
  _____

- "Whoever comes to me I will never drive away" (John 6:37).

  I used to read this verse and think that it referred to someone else. I translated it in my brain something like,

"If a murderer or a thief or an abuser comes to me, I will never drive them away." It was only after I replaced those words with my own sins that I realized the peace this verse can bring. I needed to read it, "When Laura—the adulteress, the prideful, the lost—comes to me I will never drive her away."

Try using your name and some of your sins in that verse:

When _____, the _____
_____
_____
_____

comes to me I will never drive her away."

6. Rest in God's Character

God's forgiveness flows from who He is—loving, merciful, and unchanging. Psalm 86:5 declares, "You, Lord, are forgiving and good, abounding in love to all who call to you." He's not keeping score, waiting to reject you. Instead, He's waiting with open arms to welcome you into His grace.

This is another area where God's response to us is the opposite of our responses to each other. We absolutely keep score, judge, and reject each other, and hold grudges. Because this is our instinct as human beings, it is easy to think this is God's instinct as well.

What three things does this verse say the Lord is?

_____
_____
_____

Why should those three specific attributes of the Lord give you the confidence to confess your sins to Him?

_____
_____
_____
_____

7. Live in Freedom, Not Perfection

Receiving forgiveness doesn't mean living a perfect life moving forward; it means living in the freedom of knowing your sin no longer defines you. As 2 Corinthians 5:17 reminds us, "If anyone is in Christ, the new creation has come: The old has gone, the new is here!"

This is not, however, an excuse to live in sin. Let's not pendulum swing the other direction and sin all the more, knowing that the Lord will forgive us. Paul addresses this in Romans 6:1-2, explaining, "What shall we say, then? Shall we go on sinning so that grace may increase? By no means! We are those who have died to sin; how can we live in it any longer?" For believers, we have shared in the death of Christ so we might also share in His newness of life, both in this world and in the world to come.

Are there areas of sin you still feel like you are living in? If so, list them here:

_____
_____
_____
_____

Encouragement in Community

The lie that "God can't forgive you for that" is a barrier meant to separate you from the very grace you desperately need. By recognizing the source of the lie, grounding yourself in Scripture, and trusting in Jesus' finished work, you can dismantle this untruth and step into the forgiveness and love God freely offers.

Your past doesn't define you—God's grace does. So take a step of faith, believe His promises, and walk in the assurance that nothing can separate you from His love (Romans 8:38-39).

••• Week 3 •••

The Lie:
"God Doesn't Care About You or Your Struggles"

WHERE WAS GOD when I had two miscarriages? Why did he choose to allow my grandpa to get dementia and forget who I was? Where was He during my divorce? Where was He when I would lie awake crying every night, partially because I had a newborn baby who refused to sleep and partially because I was too overwhelmed and depressed to cope?

If you're honest with yourself, you have likely asked yourself, "Where is God right now?" at least once in your life. Sometimes, He seems far away, or even non-existent. Cold. Uncaring. It feels like even if He is there and sees you, He doesn't care about you or your struggles. So, like I did, you just keep asking the questions because you're not getting any answers.

I didn't know the answer to these questions until almost a decade later. Let me rephrase: I knew the answer; I just didn't believe it. The answer, of course, is that God was always there.

According to Psalm 34:18, "The Lord is close to the brokenhearted and saves those who are crushed in spirit." He was in the hospital bed with me when I had to have my miscarried baby surgically removed. He is there holding my hand every time I visit my grandpa and he asks me what my name is. He walked beside me when I walked out of the courtroom after the divorce. He was crying by my bed all throughout those empty, lonely, sleepless nights with a screaming, inconsolable baby.

I just didn't believe that. I didn't believe it because God is not here in physical form, and my pain and struggles very much were. I didn't believe it because I was in so much emotional pain. I was blinded to the truth by my own heartache.

I know you have cried. Maybe you are crying right now. I know you have hard days. The question is not whether or not you have struggles in your life at the moment, but which struggle is the hardest. Life on this broken, sin-filled planet is tough, no question about it.

Life's hardships often plant seeds of doubt. One of the most insidious lies of Satan that can take root is the belief that *"God doesn't care about you or your struggles."* This thought can creep in during seasons of pain, silence, or unmet expectations. It is especially easy to believe if it feels like an entire season of struggle and silence.

"God Doesn't Care About You or Your Struggles"

But it is just that—a lie. Let's unpack this falsehood, examine why it arises, and uncover the truth that God's care is unwavering. His presence is constant. His love is with you, even in your darkest moments.

Why This Lie Feels True Sometimes

1. **Circumstantial Evidence**

   When life feels overwhelming—whether due to illness, financial strain, broken relationships, or unanswered prayers—it's easy to mistake hardships for God's indifference. If He is really there and He really cares, why am I going through this? Why doesn't He just solve the problem or make the pain go away? We may wrongly equate God's care with immediate relief.

   What are some things you are going through right now that feel overwhelming?

   _____
   _____
   _____
   _____

2. **Silence Feels Like Absence**

   In moments of waiting, when we don't hear from God or see tangible results, it's tempting to assume He's not listening. But silence is not the same as absence. Often, it's an invitation to deepen trust. I love the lyrics to the song *Could it Be* by Michael Card:

"Could it be, you make your presence known so often by your absence?
Could it be that questions tell us more than answers ever do?
Could it be that you would really rather die than live without us?
Could it be the only answer that means anything is you?"

I will own 100 percent that I have grown exponentially more during times of adversity than during times of peace. It's just hard to recognize that growth until after you are on the other side of that difficult season.

Can you feel God's presence right now, or does it seem like He is absent?

_____
_____

Why?

_____
_____
_____
_____

3. **Cultural Noise**

A society that prizes self-reliance often dismisses the idea of a loving, involved God. We are truly a DIY culture. Secretly, I think we are all still trying to earn God's love or acceptance. Even those of us who have accepted Christ as our Lord and Savior. When we internalize the messages all around us that "Man is the measure of all things" and that asking for help is weakness, the lie grows stronger.

In what ways are you trying to get through the struggles yourself because you are uncertain whether God is with you and at work in your life?

_____
_____
_____
_____

God's Truth About His Care

1. **Scripture Declares His Love**

   The Bible repeatedly affirms God's love and care for His people.

   - "Cast all your anxiety on Him because He cares for you" (1 Peter 5:7).

     List three things you are anxious about today that you need to give to the Lord:

     _____
     _____
     _____

   - "The Lord is near to the brokenhearted and saves the crushed in spirit" (Psalm 34:18).

     We talked about his verse earlier this week, but it is worth revisiting. Take a moment to

write out a time you were brokenhearted or crushed in spirit.

_____
_____
_____
_____

Did the Lord feel close at that time, or distant?

_____

Why do you think that was?

_____
_____
_____
_____

These verses remind us that His care isn't theoretical—it's deeply personal and active. I have felt God's hand on my shoulder and heard His voice in my heart. Each time I had an experience like that, I was physically curled up in a ball on the floor sobbing so hard I couldn't catch my breath. I take Psalm 34:18 very literally.

Write down a time the Lord felt close to you:

_____
_____
_____
_____

"God Doesn't Care About You or Your Struggles"

2. **Jesus Embodied God's Care**

   Jesus entered into human suffering to demonstrate God's compassion. His healing touch, empathy for the weary, and ultimate sacrifice on the cross affirm His profound investment in our struggles. You think God doesn't care about your struggles? He cares so much that He walked through pain Himself—excruciating, unimaginable pain—to redeem ours. Here are three specific examples of ways Jesus demonstrated how much God cares:

   Healing the Sick and Broken

   Matthew 8:1–3 states, "When Jesus came down from the mountainside, large crowds followed him. A man with leprosy came and knelt before him and said, 'Lord, if you are willing, you can make me clean.' Jesus reached out his hand and touched the man. 'I am willing,' he said. 'Be clean!' Immediately he was cleansed of his leprosy."

   Did you catch that? How did Jesus heal this man?

   _____
   _____
   _____

   The man in this passage believed that Jesus could heal him, he just didn't know if Jesus was willing to. He didn't know if Jesus truly cared about him, one man among a crowd of so many.

Have you felt like this? Like you know God is all-powerful, but maybe He isn't willing to help? Read Isaiah 64:4, "Since ancient times no one has heard, no ear has perceived, no eye has seen any God besides you, who acts on behalf of those who wait for him."

How does this verse help you interpret these feelings?

_____
_____
_____
_____

Jesus healed this man with leprosy, reaching out to touch him despite societal rejection and fear of contamination. This act not only restored the man's health but also his dignity and place in the community, demonstrating God's compassion for the marginalized.

Feeding the Hungry

John 6:1–14 states, "Some time after this, Jesus crossed to the far shore of the Sea of Galilee (that is, the Sea of Tiberias), and a great crowd of people followed him because they saw the signs he had performed by healing the sick. Then Jesus went up on a mountainside and sat down with his disciples. The Jewish Passover Festival was near.

When Jesus looked up and saw a great crowd coming toward him, he said to Philip, 'Where shall we buy bread for these people to eat?' He asked this only to test him, for he already had in mind what he was going to do.

"God Doesn't Care About You or Your Struggles"

Philip answered him, 'It would take more than half a year's wages to buy enough bread for each one to have a bite!'

Another of his disciples, Andrew, Simon Peter's brother, spoke up, 'Here is a boy with five small barley loaves and two small fish, but how far will they go among so many?'

Jesus said, 'Have the people sit down.' There was plenty of grass in that place, and they sat down (about five thousand men were there). Jesus then took the loaves, gave thanks, and distributed to those who were seated as much as they wanted. He did the same with the fish.

When they had all had enough to eat, he said to his disciples, 'Gather the pieces that are left over. Let nothing be wasted.' So they gathered them and filled twelve baskets with the pieces of the five barley loaves left over by those who had eaten."

If a crowd of over 5,000 people were following me, I can tell you I would be thinking about which one of them was going to give THEIR food to ME, not about how I could provide for THEM. That is Jesus.

Guess why those people were following Him to begin with? Sure, some of them were probably genuinely interested in His teaching, but there were probably at least a few hundred there wanting Jesus to do something for them. Wanting Him to heal them. Wanting Him to bless them. They weren't thinking about how they could serve Jesus, but Jesus was thinking about how He could serve them.

That is the glorious, upside-down way of the Gospel. The God of the universe came down to care for people who only cared about themselves. This miracle of feeding these people reflected God's care for both physical and spiritual needs, showing that He provides abundantly even when we are selfish and undeserving.

Can you think of a time when you had a physical need with no way to meet it and God stepped in to help? If so, write it here:

_____

_____

_____

_____

Comforting the Grieving

John 11:33-35 reads, "When Jesus saw her weeping, and the Jews who had come along with her also weeping, he was deeply moved in spirit and troubled. 'Where have you laid him?' he asked. 'Come and see, Lord,' they replied. Jesus wept." (For full context, read John 11:1-44.)

When Lazarus died, Jesus wept with Mary and Martha, sharing in their sorrow. He knew He was about to raise Lazarus from the dead. He knew He was about to restore the joy of the weeping sisters. Yet, in that moment, He didn't rush into the miracle of bringing Lazarus back to life. Rather, He sat and cried with the heartbroken sisters.

I think of this story when something seems to be going very, very wrong in my life, and I know God has the power to change it but doesn't seem to care or be working on it at all. Whether or not God chooses to change

"God Doesn't Care About You or Your Struggles"

my circumstances, He will always be there to cry beside me. That, all by itself, is a miracle.

What about these verses brings you the most hope right now?

_____
_____
_____
_____

3. **God Works Through Our Trials**

   While it's hard to see in the moment, God often uses struggles to grow us, refine our character, and draw us closer to Him. Romans 8:28 promises, "And we know that in all things God works for the good of those who love Him." Your pain is never wasted. In fact, it has been the very pain I have gone through that has opened doors for me to live a more vibrant, authentic, full life than I ever could have otherwise.

   Think about all the people in the Bible who endured immense pain, challenge, and struggle:

   - Noah was ridiculed by everyone for building a boat in the desert.
   - Abraham was asked to sacrifice his only son.
   - Joseph was sold into slavery and then put in prison.
   - Daniel's parents were murdered and he was taken into exile as a slave.
   - Moses was tasked with leading an entire nation of disobedient whiners around in the desert for decades.

- Paul experienced being shipwrecked, stoned, imprisoned, and beaten, just to name a few.

I could go on. Yet, where do we read that God is during each of these times?

- He is talking to Noah (Genesis 6 and 7).
- He is calling out to Abraham (Genesis 22).
- He is with Joseph (Genesis 39:2, 3, 21).
- He was with Daniel in the lion's den (Daniel 6).
- He spoke to Moses like a friend (Genesis 33:11).
- He stood near Paul in prison (Acts 23:11).

God was there with these people. He never left. I guarantee there were times when they didn't feel God. When they doubted He was at work. When He seemed silent. Yet, when I meet them in heaven, I guarantee they will all say they would gladly endure all these struggles and more to experience the presence of God in their lives.

Read the following passages and recount how the people in them experienced the presence of God:

- Isaiah 6:1-8

_____
_____
_____

- Genesis 16:7-13

_____
_____
_____

"God Doesn't Care About You or Your Struggles"

- Acts 7:54-56

The Lord cares about you and your struggles, whether it feels like it or not. Whether you believe it or not. Your belief (or lack thereof) can't change God's presence and love for you. Thank goodness for that, because I need Him with me when I can't feel Him and when I start to doubt Him. In fact, that is when I need His care the most.

How to Combat the Lie

1. **Anchor Yourself in Scripture**

   Saturate your mind with God's promises. When doubts arise, counter them with truth. Write verses on notecards, set reminders, or use them in prayer. I have a small three-ring binder with four-by-six notecards filled front and back with "Fighter Verses" and I read two each day. I have been doing this for about six years now, and every time I start to doubt God in any way, He brings one of those verses to mind.

   Here are a few to get you started:

   - **Isaiah 41:10**

     "So do not fear, for I am with you; do not be dismayed, for I am your God. I will strengthen you and help you; I will uphold you with my righteous right hand."

- **Psalm 34:18**

  "The Lord is close to the brokenhearted and saves those who are crushed in spirit."

- **1 Peter 5:7**

  "Cast all your anxiety on Him because He cares for you."

- **Matthew 10:29–31**

  "Are not two sparrows sold for a penny? Yet not one of them will fall to the ground outside your Father's care. And even the very hairs of your head are all numbered. So don't be afraid; you are worth more than many sparrows."

- **Romans 8:38–39**

  "For I am convinced that neither death nor life, neither angels nor demons, neither the present nor the future, nor any powers, neither height nor depth, nor anything else in all creation, will be able to separate us from the love of God that is in Christ Jesus our Lord."

- **Psalm 139:13–14**

  "For You created my inmost being; You knit me together in my mother's womb. I praise You because I am fearfully and wonderfully made; Your works are wonderful, I know that full well."

- **Zephaniah 3:17**

  "The Lord your God is with you, the Mighty Warrior who saves. He will take great delight in you; in His love He will no longer rebuke you, but will rejoice over you with singing."

"God Doesn't Care About You or Your Struggles"

- **Lamentations 3:22–23**
  "Because of the Lord's great love we are not consumed, for His compassions never fail. They are new every morning; great is Your faithfulness."
- **Deuteronomy 31:8**
  "The Lord Himself goes before you and will be with you; He will never leave you nor forsake you. Do not be afraid; do not be discouraged."
- **Psalm 23:1–4**
  "The Lord is my shepherd; I lack nothing. He makes me lie down in green pastures, He leads me beside quiet waters, He refreshes my soul. He guides me along the right paths for His name's sake. Even though I walk through the darkest valley, I will fear no evil, for You are with me; Your rod and Your staff, they comfort me."

2. **Recall God's Faithfulness**

   Reflect on times when God has come through for you in the past. I'm still alive, despite my best attempts during my younger years to ruin my life. Remembering all the horrible (usually self-inflicted) rough times He has brought me through gives me the perspective and confidence in Him I need to stay the course when things get rocky now. It can help to keep a gratitude journal to remind yourself of His care in small and big ways. "But the Lord is faithful, and He will strengthen you and protect you from the evil one" (2 Thessalonians 3:3).

3. **Lean on Community**

   Share your struggles with trusted friends or mentors who can remind you of God's truth when you're struggling to believe it yourself. Friends, I still need this! My friends and family still have to say things like, "Laura, maybe just pray before you respond" or, "Laura, think about it this way...." Often, God uses others to be His hands and feet and His voice of reason when I'm getting angsty over something. "And let us consider how we may spur one another on toward love and good deeds, not giving up meeting together, as some are in the habit of doing, but encouraging one another—and all the more as you see the Day approaching" (Hebrews 10:24–25).

4. **Pray Honestly**

   Bring your doubts to God. He isn't intimidated by your questions or pain. Your doubt doesn't surprise Him. He knows that our piddly, human brains cannot possibly comprehend all of who He is or what He is like or how much He loves us. Like the psalmists, pour out your heart and ask Him to help you see His care, even in the midst of trials. "I cry aloud to the Lord; I lift up my voice to the Lord for mercy. I pour out before Him my complaint; before Him I tell my trouble" (Psalm 142:1–2).

5. **Look for His Presence in the Everyday**

   God has absolutely done big, God-sized miracles in my life, and I cherish those. What means more sometimes in the grind of the everyday is when God's care shows up in unexpected ways: a timely word from a friend, a sunrise that lifts your spirit, or peace in a moment of chaos. Open your eyes to these whispers of His love. "God has said, 'Never will I leave you; never will I forsake you.' So we say with confidence, 'The Lord is my helper; I will not be afraid'" (Hebrews 13:5–6).

6. **The Truth That Sets You Free**

"God Doesn't Care About You or Your Struggles"

The lie that God doesn't care about you or your struggles is a trap meant to isolate you from His love. But the truth is, God's care is constant, steadfast, and more intimate than you can imagine. He sees every tear (Psalm 56:8), carries your burdens (Matthew 11:28-30), and works tirelessly for your good. Reject the lie and hold fast to the truth: God deeply cares for you and your struggles—not because of what you do, but because of who He is. You are loved, seen, and held by the One who has promised never to leave you or forsake you. Lean into His care today and let His truth anchor your soul.

When I start to think God doesn't care about me, I think of one of the first songs I sang as a child in Sunday school, "Jesus Loves the Little Children." A familiar favorite written by Clarence Herbert Woolston, the words to the chorus of this song are simple, but the message communicates a very deep truth:

> *Jesus loves the little children,*
> *All the children of the world.*
> *Red and yellow, black and white,*
> *All are precious in His sight,*
> *Jesus loves the little children of the world.*[2]

You are precious in His sight, friend. Remember that always.

••• Week 4 •••

The Lie:
"Your Worth Is Based on Your Performance or Appearance"

I'M PRETTY SURE Satan devised this lie specifically for me. I'm a firstborn, and every personality test I've ever taken (close to fifteen) has told me the same thing: I'm a perfectionist. I like things done a certain way. I set expectations for myself and others that are impossible to achieve. In my head, we all should be amazing employees, mothers, wives, sisters, friends, and human beings, all while looking gorgeous, having spotless houses, and getting eight hours of sleep at night. Clearly, I am delusional. This lie works on me most days.

"Your Worth Is Based on Your Performance or Appearance"

Yet, somehow, I still get upset with anyone (myself included) who does not live up to my standards. From the beginning, Satan has used lies to distort our understanding of who we are and where our worth lies. One of his most pervasive deceptions is this: *"Your worth is based on your performance or appearance."* It's a falsehood that enslaves us in a relentless cycle of striving and self-doubt.

But as followers of Christ, we are called to reject this lie and anchor our identity in God's truth. Left to myself, I would be a ball of rage, rolling over everyone and everything less than ideal in my path. No one wants to be around a rage ball.

The Lie in Light of Scripture

This lie echoes Satan's tactics in the Garden of Eden. He convinced Eve that what she *did*—eating the forbidden fruit—could elevate her worth by making her "like God." Genesis 3:5 says, "For God knows that when you eat from it your eyes will be opened, and you will be like God, knowing good and evil." He convinced her that she could elevate her performance and power and become better. Become worth more.

Of course, God knew what would happen when Eve ate the fruit. He told her very clearly. "But you must not eat from the tree of the knowledge of good and evil, for when you eat from it you will certainly die" (Genesis 2:17). God told Eve if she ate the fruit, she would die. Satan told her if she ate the fruit, she would be "like God." At some point, Eve must have decided that the chance to be "like God" was worth the risk of death. How badly must she have wanted to be powerful?

All-knowing? Perfect? Badly enough to put her own life on the line.

Did eating the fruit allow Eve to know good and evil? Yes. Did it make her like God? Not in the way she wanted. I once heard the following quote from a pastor: "Sin takes you farther than you want to go, keeps you longer than you want to stay, and costs you more than you want to pay." I have never forgotten it because it is true. All the time, every time. Eve paid the dearest of prices for wanting to perfect. Wanting to be "like God."

In the same way, Satan whispers to us that we must perform better, look perfect, or achieve more to have value. He gets me to believe all the time that I am failing at something because I'm not perfect in that area. If I'm not perfect, I'm not valuable or lovable. Yet, the Bible speaks a radically different truth: our worth is not earned but given, rooted in the unchanging love of our Creator.

Consider the words of the psalmist:

"For you created my inmost being; you knit me together in my mother's womb. I praise you because I am fearfully and wonderfully made" (Psalm 139:13–14).

This verse reminds us that our value comes from being made in the image of God, as the Bible says in Genesis 1:27, "So God created mankind in his own image, in the image of God he created them; male and female he created them." It has nothing to do with how we look or what we achieve. If I never got out of bed this morning, I would not have lost any value to the Lord because I was unproductive.

"Your Worth Is Based on Your Performance or Appearance"

Some of the best prayer warriors I know who are moving heaven and earth with their petitions to the Lord are on bed rest or confined mostly to a chair. Rather, our value has everything to do with the One who created us.

The Danger of Believing the Lie

When we believe our worth is tied to performance or appearance, we live as slaves to approval—whether from people, society, or even ourselves. This mindset can lead to exhaustion, insecurity, and despair.

I'm sure by now you have a mental image of me zipping around trying to accomplish all the things until eventually I get going so fast I explode. Literally, I don't explode. Metaphorically, I do. When I get so worn down from going, going, going, and trying to accomplish everything to prove my worth, I will have a breakdown at some point.

It may be a physical breakdown, like when the IT band in my left knee got all out of whack because I didn't take the time to stretch or cross-train when I would go for a run. It might be an emotional breakdown, like when I just burst into tears for no reason at all when I see a picture of a cute puppy. It could be a mental breakdown, like when my brain takes a vacation, and I forget I signed up to take a meal to a friend who just had a baby, or I forget it's my anniversary, or I forget to turn off the water when I finish the dishes. Individually, these occurrences are understandable. When all three happen in the same day, it may be a sign that my brain is having a breakdown.

Jesus warned about the emptiness of living for human approval: "What good is it for someone to gain the whole world, yet forfeit their soul?" (Mark 8:36). If we spend our lives chasing success or beauty, we risk losing sight of the eternal truth: our identity is found in Christ, not in the fleeting standards of the world.

The Truth About Worth in Christ

The gospel declares our worth is not based on what we do but on what Christ has done for us. At the cross, Jesus paid the ultimate price for our sins, declaring us worthy of His love and grace. As Paul writes,

"But God demonstrates his own love for us in this: While we were still sinners, Christ died for us" (Romans 5:8).

What did Christ do for us according to this verse?

_____

_____

When did He do this according to that verse?

_____

_____

Can you imagine giving your life for someone else? I would give my life for my kids or my husband without thinking twice. But what about someone who had done many, many, many bad things? Would I give my life for a liar, a cheater, and a thief? Jesus did. That is exactly who I was, and Jesus died for me, knowing that I would commit those horrible sins and countless more.

He didn't do it because I recognized my sins and my need for Him, cried out to Him for help, and promised to spend my life serving Him. Rather, He sought me out when I was running away from Him and breaking His heart—when I had nothing to offer Him but ruin and brokenness.

Friends, this verse changed my life. It means our value is secure, not because of anything we can achieve, but because of God's unchanging love. Wait, what? I don't have to be the best at everything for God to love me? Then why is my default habit to live like if I'm not achieving, I'm not loved by Him or anyone else? Lies of Satan. That's why.

Here's the truth. In Christ, we are:

- **Chosen**: "For he chose us in him before the creation of the world to be holy and blameless in his sight" (Ephesians 1:4).

    How does it make you feel to know that if you are a believer, God chose you?

    _____
    _____
    _____
    _____

- **Loved**: "See what great love the Father has lavished on us, that we should be called children of God!" (1 John 3:1).

What has the Father done with His love?

_____
_____

What are we called as believers?

_____
_____

What does it mean to you to know God considers you His child?

_____
_____
_____
_____

- **Accepted**: "There is now no condemnation for those who are in Christ Jesus" (Romans 8:1).

    How much condemnation is there for you if you have asked Jesus to be your savior?

    _____

    What does it mean to you to know you are accepted by God?

    _____
    _____
    _____
    _____

"Your Worth Is Based on Your Performance or Appearance"

How to Reject the Lie

1. **Renew Your Mind with God's Word**

    To combat Satan's lies, we must immerse ourselves in Scripture. Meditate on verses that affirm your identity in Christ, such as Ephesians 2:10: "For we are God's handiwork, created in Christ Jesus to do good works, which God prepared in advance for us to do."

    What are we, according to that verse?

    _____
    _____

    What are we created to do?

    _____
    _____

    Are we left alone to try to figure out these good works?

    _____

    You mean we are handiwork? Think of a master artist painting a masterpiece, a master baker decorating a cake, or a master musician composing a symphony. God thinks of you as His masterpiece.

    He has really created us for good works? Some days, it doesn't feel like that. That doesn't mean it isn't the truth. Guess what, He "prepared in advance" for us to do these good works. That means you don't have to have everything all planned out. God already does. Our job is not to come up with the plan, but to follow His plan.

2. **Rest in Grace, Not Striving**

    Your worth isn't earned by what you do; it's a gift from God. Embrace the truth of Matthew 11:28–30: "Come to me, all you who are weary and burdened, and I will give you rest. Take my yoke upon you and learn from me, for I am gentle and humble in heart, and you will find rest for your souls. For my yoke is easy and my burden is light."

    You know what makes me truly weary and burdened? Trying to earn the love and approval of God and others. Constantly striving to achieve things. To look great, have a clean house, be present for others, and raise my children well. Recognizing your value in God will give you rest from having to maintain the façade of perfection to earn value.

List some things you do to try to earn love and approval:

_____

_____

_____

_____

3. **Focus on the Heart, Not the Outward Appearance**

    God doesn't measure us by the world's standards. As He told Samuel: "The Lord does not look at the things people look at. People look at the outward appearance, but the Lord looks at the heart" (1 Samuel 16:7). Let your inner character and relationship with Christ take

"Your Worth Is Based on Your Performance or Appearance"

precedence over external appearances. Ladies, outward beauty fades. (Let's be honest, though, that doesn't stop me from using retinol and hyaluronic acid creams!) Inner beauty, however, can grow with age if we will surrender to the sanctification of the Lord. I, for one, want to age gracefully inwardly and outwardly.

List some ways you can focus on growing your inner beauty:

_____
_____
_____
_____

4. **Anchor Your Identity in Christ**

   Instead of seeking validation from others, remember who you are in Christ.

   "And he died for all, that those who live should no longer live for themselves but for him who died for them and was raised again. So from now on we regard no one from a worldly point of view. Though we once regarded Christ in this way, we do so no longer. Therefore, if anyone is in Christ, the new creation has come: The old has gone, the new is here!" (2 Corinthians 5:17).

   What happened to the old you when you accepted Christ as your savior according to those verses?

   _____
   _____
   _____
   _____

The old is gone. Not like hidden away in a top cupboard waiting to come out again in a secret moment like my stash of sour patch kids candy, but gone. Like thrown in the trash can, taken to the dump, and incinerated, never to be seen again. Like when you exfoliate and the dead skin cells fall off so new ones can take their place. Let's not walk around with a bunch of dead skin hanging on. Off with the old and on with the new!

What are some ways you may be still hanging on to old ways of trying to find worth based on performance or appearance?

_____
_____
_____
_____

Living in Freedom

The lie that your worth is based on performance or appearance is a mask meant to keep you blind to hope. But Christ came to set you free: "Then you will know the truth, and the truth will set you free" (John 8:32). Ladies, if the Lord has set us free, let's not put ourselves or our fellow women back in bondage by judging based on performance or appearance. We all have those days where we feel like a rat pulled through a knothole backward. Solidarity, sisters.

When you reject this lie and embrace God's truth, you'll find freedom from striving, freedom from insecurity, and freedom to live as the person God created you to be. Your worth is not earned; it's established by the One who loves you unconditionally. Let this truth shape your life today.

··· Week 5 ···

The Lie: "God Isn't Fair"

HAVE YOU EVER thought, "Why did that amazing thing happen to her? That sort of thing never happens to me. God must love her more than me. He isn't fair." I think this when I see pictures on social media of my friends doing super cool things on vacation. For some reason, it seems all my friends are constantly on vacation. Everyone is on a beach in Florida right now. They are not actually; I just feel that way because those are the pictures I like to look at the most.

Or have you thought, "Why is this terrible thing happening to me? I always seem to get more than my fair share of adversity. God isn't fair." I felt this way when my kid broke his arm a few days before his birthday, and I found out a close friend had a heart attack, and my husband was laid off. Life seemed very unfair then.

One of Satan's most persistent lies is this: *"God isn't fair."* It's a seed of doubt meant to make us question God's goodness, His justice, and His plans for our lives. Whether it's through unmet expectations, suffering, or watching others prosper while we struggle, this lie can feel convincing. But as with all of Satan's deceptions, it collapses under the truth of God's Word.

The Origin of the Lie

This lie is as old as humanity. Let's go back to the Garden of Eden again. This lie of Satan was planted when he told Eve, "Did God really say you must not eat from any tree in the garden?" (Genesis 3:1). Satan implied that God was withholding something good, painting Him as unjust or unfair. Eve believed the lie, doubted God's character, and acted in disobedience.

Ladies, let's get real here. I used to be so offended that Eve doubted God and chose to believe a lie of Satan and give in to sin. Gee, thanks, girl. You cursed the rest of us for thousands of years. Way to give women a bad name. I used to think if I could go back in time and take Eve's place, I could be the one to say no to Satan and spare humanity thousands of years of the curse of sin.

Guess what? If it had been me in the Garden of Eden that day, I would have made the same choice as Eve. I would have given in to the lie of Satan at some point. Maybe not the first time, but at some point, I would have eaten the fruit too. How do I know this? Because I have also chosen to believe this lie of Satan and give in to sin. More than once. More than a hundred times. Who am I to judge Eve? The problem is that the result of believing God is not fair, just as it was with Eve, is brokenness and separation from God.

How crazy is it that Satan is still using the same tactics today that he used in the garden? The even crazier part is they still work. Satan wants us to fixate on what we don't have, what's going wrong, or what feels unfair rather than on God's faithfulness and love.

Why the Lie Feels Convincing

1. **Life's Injustices**

    From personal struggles to global tragedies, it's easy to feel like life isn't fair. We all have moments, days, even years of adversity. Satan twists these moments to suggest God is to blame. After all, if God is really in control, and He really loves us, why is He allowing all these bad things to happen?

2. **Comparison**

    When we see others succeeding or enjoying the blessings we crave, we might wonder why God hasn't done the same for us. I have thought, "I have a better attendance record at church than she does. Why is her business thriving while mine is struggling? Why isn't God blessing me when I'm trying to serve Him?" Um, perhaps because God is not a vending machine where you can make a specific deposit in the form of church attendance or Bible reading and expect Him to dispense something like business success (or health or great relationships or popularity, etc.) in return. Comparison only breeds discontentment and doubt.

3. **Limited Perspective**

   Our view of fairness is often shaped by immediate circumstances. We struggle to understand how God's eternal plans are working for our good in the midst of pain or waiting. Pain is one of the biggest blinders I know of, and it robs us of hope and joy. When you look at your life and it doesn't seem fair, it may be because you're looking through the wrong lens. Here are a few examples from the world of science:

   - A survey by the Mental Health Foundation found that fifty-one percent of adults who felt stressed reported feeling depressed, and sixty-one percent reported feeling anxious. Additionally, thirty-seven percent of those experiencing stress felt lonely as a result.[3]
   - According to *ScienceDaily*, individuals who experienced multiple adversities in adulthood had a twenty-four percent higher chance of depression and also experienced cognitive decline.[4]
   - Research published in *Frontiers in Psychology* indicates that childhood adversity is associated with cognitive impairment in later life. The study examined indicators such as grade retention, parental substance abuse, and physical abuse, finding a correlation between early-life adversity and later cognitive challenges.[5]

   Overcoming the lie that "God isn't fair" can be increasingly difficult the more trauma you have experienced. Even when God does not seem fair, the fact that He is doesn't change. Our perspective, limited by our humanity and our struggles, often just cannot grasp that.

The Truth About God's Fairness

The truth is that life is not fair. We are not all created equally, treated equally, or born into equal circumstances. Some were born with congenital anomalies, to abusive parents, or into poverty. Others were born exceptionally beautiful to loving parents who own billion-dollar companies. Some people are treated like royalty, while others are bullied. There is only one thing every human who has ever been born has in common: We are all born sinners.

The most unfair part of all is God chooses to pursue and forgive sinners who openly reject and refuse Him. Sinners like me. If God were a fair God, I would be doomed to an eternity in hell. There wouldn't be any common grace on this earth, like unbelievers who find happy marriages or raise incredible children. It's not fair that humans who reject God should find any measure of comfort or joy in this life. I am so grateful that God is not fair.

I once heard this quote by R.C. Sproul (one of my favorites!): "When I think I am unfairly hated, I try to remember that I am unfairly loved." The more we read God's Word, the more we can see how He reveals His true character, and it dismantles Satan's lie.

1. **God Is Just**

    "He is the Rock, His works are perfect, and all His ways are just. A faithful God who does no wrong, upright and just is He" (Deuteronomy 32:4).

What two words are used in this verse to describe the works and ways of God?

_____
_____

What five things does this verse say God is?

_____
_____
_____
_____
_____

What descriptive word is used twice in that verse?

_____

"If we confess our sins, he is faithful and just and will forgive us our sins and purify us from all unrighteousness" (1 John 1:9).

What two things does this verse say God is?

_____
_____

What two things does this verse say God will do for us if we confess our sins?

_____
_____

Here is the real question: How can a God who is just forgive sins? Sins deserve to be punished. While the answer to this question is quite lengthy, I think a summary here would be helpful to reorient our perspective on the fairness of God.

God's Justice Requires a Payment for Sin
God is perfectly just and holy, meaning He cannot overlook sin without violating His own nature. Sin carries a penalty, which is separation from God, as the Bible says in the first part of Romans 6:23: "For the wages of sin is death…." Justice demands that this penalty be paid, ensuring that God's moral law is upheld.

God's Mercy Provides a Way
While justice requires punishment, God's mercy makes a way for forgiveness without compromising His justice. How, you ask? This is accomplished through Jesus Christ, who took the penalty for sin upon Himself. In 2 Corinthians 5:21, the Bible says, "God made him who had no sin to be sin for us, so that in him we might become the righteousness of God."

Jesus' death on the cross was the ultimate act of substitution, satisfying God's justice while extending mercy to humanity. Did you read that? "Him who had no sin" was made "to be sin for us." For me. For you. Does that seem fair? Not at all, and I will spend eternity thanking and praising God for it.

The Cross Unites Justice and Forgiveness
At the cross, God's justice and mercy meet. Romans 3:25–26 explains this. "God presented Christ as a sacrifice of atonement, through the shedding of his

blood—to be received by faith. He did this to demonstrate his righteousness, because in his forbearance he had left the sins committed beforehand unpunished— he did it to demonstrate his righteousness at the present time, so as to be just and the one who justifies those who have faith in Jesus."

This verse shares that God presented Jesus as a sacrifice for sin to demonstrate His justice and allow Him to be both "just and the one who justifies those who have faith in Jesus." By placing faith in Jesus, we can receive forgiveness because the penalty for sin has already been paid. The debt we owed was erased. Our sins are no more, and we didn't do anything—couldn't do anything—to accomplish that. Again, this doesn't seem fair.

Forgiveness Offered Freely, Received by Faith

God's forgiveness is not arbitrary; it is grounded in the finished work of Christ. This forgiveness is offered to all but must be received by faith, as the Bible says in Ephesians 2:8–9. "For it is by grace you have been saved, through faith—and this is not from yourselves, it is the gift of God— not by works, so that no one can boast."

Hmmm, it kind of sounds like the Lord knew people would try to claim that they are good enough to earn salvation on their own. I wouldn't know *anything* about that. (Can you tell that's sarcasm?) Those who repent and trust in Jesus are justified—declared righteous before God—because their sins are fully dealt with through Christ's sacrifice.

God's justice is not compromised in forgiving sins because the penalty for sin is paid by Jesus. His mercy and grace make forgiveness possible. Not our striving.

Not our "good" deeds. Not our acts of service to Him. This reality reflects the depth of His love and the perfection of His character. God's justice is perfect, even when we don't see it fully. His timing and plans extend beyond our understanding.

2. **God's Grace Goes Beyond Fairness**

    If God operated solely on fairness, none of us would be saved, because we all fall short of His glory. As the Bible says in Romans 3:23, "For all have sinned and fall short of the glory of God." But in His mercy, He gives us grace we don't deserve: "For the wages of sin is death, but the gift of God is eternal life in Christ Jesus our Lord." Amen!

3. **God's Plans Are Higher**

    "For my thoughts are not your thoughts, neither are your ways my ways," declares the Lord (Isaiah 55:8). We may not always understand God's actions, but we can trust His wisdom and love. He may not seem fair, but things aren't always what they seem.

How to Overcome This Lie

Spoiler alert: this is not a lie you can overcome once and be done with. It will continue to crop up. The good news is that the more often you defeat this lie, the easier it gets to do it in the future.

1. **Focus on God's Character**

    Spend time in Scripture to remind yourself of God's faithfulness, love, and justice. Verses like Psalm 145:17 ("The Lord is righteous in all His ways and faithful in all He does") reaffirm who He is.

Describe three times you saw God demonstrate His faithfulness, love, and mercy to you:

_____
_____
_____
_____
_____

2. Choose Gratitude Over Comparison

Instead of focusing on what feels unfair in a negative way, thank God for what is unfair in a positive way—all the ways He has unfairly blessed you. Gratitude shifts your perspective and reminds you of God's goodness.

Read 2 Corinthians 9:8-10. Write what you learn about the blessings of God:

_____
_____
_____
_____
_____

3. Trust God's Eternal Perspective

Life on earth is temporary, but God's plans are eternal. What feels unfair now will make sense in the fullness of His kingdom. (Boy, this is a tough one for me! I want to see it now!) "I consider that our present sufferings are not worth comparing with the glory that will be revealed in us" (Romans 8:18).

"God Isn't Fair"

Read Revelation 21:1-4. What about this description of heaven is most exciting to you?

_____
_____
_____
_____

4. Bring Your Doubts to God

It's okay to feel confused or frustrated. Bring your questions to God in prayer. The psalmists often cried out in honesty, and God met them with His presence and reassurance. I will advise against throwing a temper tantrum at God, though. I have never come away from that feeling good about myself. He is still the God of the universe and should be approached with respect and reverence, even when we're angry or hurt or frustrated.

Read Psalm 42. What gives the writer hope even though life seems unfair?

_____
_____
_____
_____

5. Look to Jesus

Jesus endured the ultimate "unfairness" when He took on the sins of the world, though He was blameless. You want to talk about not fair to God? Go ahead. He never did anything wrong, yet took the blame, the torture, the humiliation, and the death that we deserved. That I deserved. That you deserved. He gets your feelings that "life is not fair." He died so you don't have to be a slave to that lie of Satan. His sacrifice reminds us God's ways are not about fairness by human standards but about redeeming love and grace.

Read 1 Corinthians 15:55-57. What is ours through the Lord Jesus Christ?

_____

_____

Living in the Truth

When Satan whispers, *"God isn't fair,"* counter the lie with faith. Remember that God's ways are just, His grace is abundant, and His plans are for your ultimate good. Trusting Him doesn't mean life will always make sense, but it does mean you can rest in the truth of His character.

The next time you're tempted to believe the lie, reflect on this: God's fairness isn't about giving us what we think we deserve—it's about giving us more than we could ever ask or imagine through His mercy and love.

"The Lord is compassionate and gracious, slow to anger, abounding in love" (Psalm 103:8).

··· Week 6 ···

The Lie:
"Your Past Defines You"

LET ME SHARE with you a bit about past Laura. Past Laura was selfish with her time and tended to prioritize herself and her tasks over relationships with others. She thought she knew better than others and let pride get the best of her. This Laura had a hard time admitting she was wrong or saying, "I'm sorry." Just to clarify, by "past" Laura I mean the person I was five minutes ago. These are the sins I struggle with on a daily basis.

If we go further back, I can share stories of my past life where I told whopper lies, cheated on my spouse, stole from the company I worked for, and drove drunk. This Laura is someone I am ashamed of and embarrassed to talk about. I will never forget the night all the guilt I shoved down when I was engaging in these sins came bubbling to the surface.

I had separated from my husband and was living with another man. Then I found out that man was cheating on me. This was a low point for me. I stopped eating because my stomach was in such knots I couldn't choke down food. I stopped working because I couldn't function in a professional setting, and I spent all day in bed. I couldn't sleep much. All I could do was cry.

I cried for the shame I felt (finally) for all the sins I had been accumulating without confession or remorse. I cried for all the friendships I had stepped on and used in an attempt to be popular and make myself feel important or pretty. I cried for the family I hadn't talked to in months and missed terribly. I cried for all my hopes and dreams for what my life and future would look like that now seemed gone for good.

After ten days, I had some decisions to make. Obviously, staying in bed and crying was not a sustainable lifestyle. I had to move on. But how? I spent another few days at home answering that question. The decision to reinvent myself was not my own (most great ones aren't), but it was the voice of the Lord telling me that He created me for more than the person I had been living as.

Along my journey since then, it has been a struggle not to give in to one of Satan's most paralyzing lies: *"Your past defines you."* This deception is designed to keep us shackled by guilt, shame, and regret, convincing us that our mistakes, failures, or wounds are permanent barriers to living in God's purpose. But the truth of Scripture tells a different story—one of grace, transformation, and freedom.

"Your Past Defines You"

The Power of the Lie

Satan thrives on using our past to distort how we see ourselves and God. We all have a past we aren't proud of. Whether your past is as dramatic as mine, or if my past makes yours look like a picnic, we are all sinners with a rap sheet. Here's how Satan does it:

1. **Shame Over Sins**

    He whispers, *"Look at what you've done. God can't love someone like you."* This lie can lead us to feel unworthy of God's forgiveness and grace. The trick is to learn the difference between guilt and shame.

    As we talked about in Week 2 with the lie, "God can't forgive you for that," guilt is a good thing designed by God to keep us from making unwise decisions or to alert us when we have already made them. Shame is a tool Satan uses to keep us from reaching out for help.

    The following is one of my favorite verses on shame: "Rather, we have renounced secret and shameful ways; we do not use deception, nor do we distort the word of God. On the contrary, by setting forth the truth plainly, we commend ourselves to everyone's conscience in the sight of God" (2 Corinthians 4:2).

    What have we done to secret and shameful ways according to this verse?

    _____
    _____
    _____

If you have truly renounced and rejected your past sins, they no longer have any power over you.

2. **Shame About Identity**

   He says, *"You'll never change. Who you were is who you are."* Satan tries to make us believe our identity is forever tied to our worst moments. I will never forget my worst moments. They are a part of me. Now, rather than looking back on those in shame, I look back and see that those were the times when the Lord loved me the most and was working hard to draw me back to Himself. Here are truths from Scripture about your identity in Christ.

   You Are a Child of God

   Christians are adopted into God's family and are His beloved children.

   "See what great love the Father has lavished on us, that we should be called children of God! And that is what we are!" (1 John 3:1).

   "The Spirit you received brought about your adoption to sonship. And by Him, we cry, 'Abba, Father'" (Romans 8:15).

   According to Logos Bible Software, the term "Abba, Father" used in Romans 8:15 is considered by some scholars "to be a colloquial term of familiarity that a young child would have used, similar to how American children use 'papa' or 'daddy.'"

"Your Past Defines You"

As a child of God, how can you talk to God according to that verse?

_____
_____
_____

Forgiven and Redeemed

We are forgiven of our sins and redeemed through Jesus' sacrifice.

"In Him, we have redemption through His blood, the forgiveness of sins, in accordance with the riches of God's grace" (Ephesians 1:7).

In addition to being forgiven and redeemed, what else do we have in Christ according to this verse?

_____
_____

Righteous and Justified

Through faith in Christ, Christians are declared righteous before God.

"This righteousness is given through faith in Jesus Christ to all who believe" (Romans 3:22). According to the Merriam-Webster Dictionary, righteousness is defined as, "acting in accord with divine or moral law: free from guilt or sin."[6]

Write your thoughts about what it means to be "free from guilt."

_____
_____
_____
_____

Ambassadors for Christ

Christians are representatives of Jesus in the world. "We are therefore Christ's ambassadors, as though God were making His appeal through us" (2 Corinthians 5:20). Think about it this way: If you were the only Christian someone were to ever meet, what would that person's opinion of God be after meeting you?

How can you approach every interaction as an opportunity to represent Christ well?

_____
_____
_____
_____

Citizens of Heaven

As Christians, our ultimate home is in heaven, not on earth.

"But our citizenship is in heaven. And we eagerly await a Savior from there, the Lord Jesus Christ" (Philippians 3:20). Someday, all we will be able to focus on is glorifying God. If our past will not be our focus in heaven, it should not be our focus here on earth.

"Your Past Defines You"

What does it mean to you to know you are already a citizen of heaven if you are a believer in Christ?

_____
_____
_____
_____

Members of Christ's Body

Believers are part of a spiritual family united in Christ.

"Now you are the body of Christ, and each one of you is a part of it" (1 Corinthians 12:27). Sometimes I feel like the armpit of the body of Christ, or maybe the smallest toe. Smelly, gross, unnoticed, unappreciated. I want to be the eyes or the mouth. Something appealing or important. The truth is I would rather be an armpit in the body of Christ than the lush hair or sparkling eyes in any other body. Regardless of what you feel your function is in the body, you are an integral part of the most important body in creation.

What importance, privilege, and responsibility do you think you have as part of the body of Christ?

_____
_____
_____
_____
_____
_____

Salt and Light of the World

Christians are called to influence the world positively and shine God's truth.

"You are the salt of the earth. But if the salt loses its saltiness, how can it be made salty again? It is no longer good for anything, except to be thrown out and trampled underfoot. "You are the light of the world. A town built on a hill cannot be hidden" (Matthew 5:13-14). What does salt do? It makes us thirsty. I cannot eat even a small bag of McDonald's French fries without needing a drink of water.

Read Jeremiah 2:13. What does this verse say that God is?

_____

If God is the living water, and Christians are the salt of the earth, I think that means we are called to make people thirst after and yearn for God. Want to know Him and have more of Him.

What do you think our job is as "the light of the world"?

_____
_____
_____
_____

Heirs of God

Christians share in God's inheritance through Christ. "Now if we are children, then we are heirs—heirs of God and co-heirs with Christ" (Romans 8:17). Think of everything Christ receives in heaven. According to this verse, not only can we look forward to a future in heaven, but we are also considered co-heirs with Christ there.

Take some time to do research on your own about what a co-heir receives. What do you think this means for you?

_____
_____
_____
_____
_____
_____
_____
_____

Holy and Set Apart

Christians are called to live holy lives, set apart for God.

"But you are a chosen people, a royal priesthood, a holy nation, God's special possession" (1 Peter 2:9).

What does it mean to you that God considers you His "special possession"?

_____
_____
_____
_____

The Bible affirms that Christians are deeply loved, redeemed, and called to live in a way that reflects their new identity in Christ. This identity is grounded in God's grace and His purpose for their lives. In a world where you can choose to identify as just about anything, I am so glad the Lord has given us a very clear sense of identity!

3. **Fear of Moving Forward**

    He uses our past as a weapon to create fear, saying, *"If people knew the real you, they'd reject you."* This keeps us isolated and stuck. Yes, people might reject you when they hear your story. Or, the story of your past could be the exact thing they needed to hear in order to break through the secret sins they have been struggling with.

    Who do you know that might be encouraged by your story and your past?

    _____
    _____
    _____
    _____

The Truth About Your Past

God's Word dismantles Satan's lies and reveals how we can overcome them:

1. **Your Past Is Forgiven**

    "If we confess our sins, He is faithful and just and will forgive us our sins and purify us from all unrighteousness" (1 John 1:9).

"Your Past Defines You"

Through Christ's sacrifice, your sins are not just covered—they're erased. God doesn't hold your past against you. Not just the "small" sins of bad attitudes or taking a few too many days to forgive someone. He forgives even the "big" sins of adultery, stealing, and lying.

List some specific sins that God has forgiven you for:

_____
_____
_____

2. **You Are a New Creation**

   "Therefore, if anyone is in Christ, the new creation has come: The old has gone, the new is here!" (2 Corinthians 5:17).

   In Christ, your identity is no longer defined by your past but by His righteousness. You are not your mistakes—you are redeemed and made new. You have only to look as far as the people in the Bible to see that this is true. Look at Joseph's pride as a boy. Look at King David's adultery and murder. Look at Rahab's prostitution. Look at Moses's murder. Look at Sarah's unbelief. These are heroes of the faith, and their pasts were sketchy at best. This is good news for you and me!

   Who is someone in the Bible with a past that you can relate to?

   _____

3. **God Works All Things for Good**

   "And we know that in all things God works for the good of those who love Him, who have been called according to His purpose" (Romans 8:28). God can take even the most painful parts of your past and use them for His glory and your growth. While this verse can be taken out of context, I also love the verse Genesis 50:20 that says, "You meant evil against me, but God meant it for good" (ESV). Again, sometimes it is the most painful times that bring us back into right relationship with the Lord.

   Think of a time in your life where you or someone else did something intending evil, but the Lord used it for good.

   _____
   _____
   _____
   _____

How to Overcome This Lie

1. **Anchor Your Identity in Christ**

   Meditate on who God says you are: forgiven, loved, chosen, and redeemed. Memorize Scriptures like Ephesians 1:4–5 that affirm your identity in Him.

   Write out those verses here:

   _____
   _____

"Your Past Defines You"

_____
_____

2. **Confess and Surrender Your Past**

   Lay your past at the feet of Jesus. Acknowledge your sins, regrets, or pain, and trust that His grace is sufficient. Once confessed, refuse to pick it back up—it's forgiven.

   Take the time to write down any unconfessed sins or sins you are currently struggling with. Ask forgiveness and then use this as a line in the sand to know it has been forgiven.

   _____
   _____
   _____
   _____

3. **Refuse to Let Shame Speak**

   When shame tries to creep in, respond with God's truth. Say aloud, "There is now no condemnation for those who are in Christ Jesus" (Romans 8:1).

   Write, "no condemnation, no shame" seven times:

   _____
   _____
   _____
   _____
   _____

4. Share Your Story for God's Glory

Satan wants you to hide your past, but God can use it to encourage others. Your testimony of how God has redeemed your life can bring hope and healing to someone else. It may seem like burying your past will make you seem like a better person, but those skeletons have a way of being dug up eventually anyway. Don't let them rot in your closet and infect other areas. Getting the rot of your past out in the open will prevent it from coming back to haunt you.

What is something that you are embarrassed or ashamed of that you can talk to God about and share with a trusted friend or family member?

_____
_____
_____
_____

5. Trust God's Purpose for Your Future

Don't let your past hold you back from stepping into the plans God has for you. Lamentations 3:22–23 says, "Because of the Lord's great love we are not consumed, for his compassions never fail. They are new every morning; great is your faithfulness."

When do His compassions fail?

_____

When are they new?

_____

"Your Past Defines You"

According to Jeremiah 29:11, "For I know the plans I have for you,' declares the Lord, 'plans to prosper you and not to harm you, plans to give you hope and a future.'"

What does God have for us?

_____

What kind of plans?

_____

Living in Freedom

The enemy wants to keep you bound by your past, but Christ came to set you free. Satan knows that if you are hiding in shame, you cannot be outspoken for Christ. He wants you to listen to him and his lie. Today is the day to tell him to shut up. The cross is proof your sins and failures don't have the final word—Jesus does.

When Satan whispers, *"Your past defines you,"* you just tell him with confidence: *"I am defined by the love and grace of Jesus Christ, and in Him, I am a new creation."* Walk in the freedom of God's truth, knowing that your past is not your identity. It's part of your story, but it doesn't determine your destiny.

··· Week 7 ···

The Lie: "You Can Do This On Your Own"

THIS IS ANOTHER one of those lies that I have to fight against every day. In my head, I am a strong, independent woman, and I can do all the things by myself. This looks like me strutting around with my head held high, changing the lightbulbs and the air filters, gluing the kids' broken toys back together, and sewing their torn pants (why is it always the pants?) while singing the lyrics to the Frank Sinatra song, *My Way*:

> "I did what I had to do
> And saw it through without exemption
> I planned each charted course
> Each careful step along the byway

"You Can Do This On Your Own"

> And more, much more than this
> I did it my way!"

Then, as the day (or the project I'm working on) progresses, my confidence usually transitions. I drop a light bulb, super-glue my finger to the toy I'm trying to fix, and lose my sewing needle down the couch. By the end of the day, I look more like Squidward Tentacles from SpongeBob SquarePants, all mopey and forlorn and singing something more like Celine Dion's *All By Myself*:

> "Hard to be sure
> Sometimes, I feel so insecure
> And love's so distant and obscure
> Remains the cure
>
> All by myself
> Don't wanna be
> All by myself
> Anymore"

One of Satan's subtle but dangerous lies is *"You can do this on your own."* It sounds empowering, even noble, but at its heart, it's a strategy to isolate us from God and others—to separate us from the proverbial pack so we are easier to take down. Without support and encouragement from family and friends, we are weaker and more vulnerable.

I tend to believe this lie because it feeds my pride. "Look how great I am! See what I did all on my own! I'm so capable!" Believing this lie not only keeps us from accomplishing more, but weakens our dependence on God, and leaves us spiritually vulnerable. To overcome it, we must root ourselves in God's truth and design for our lives.

The Power of the Lie

As I have mentioned before, the lies of Satan are powerful because they are partly true. There are some things we can do by ourselves. But just because we can doesn't mean we should. Would you rather bake cookies by yourself or with your friends or kids? Would you rather watch a movie by yourself or with your family? Would you rather work alone or with a partner? We can do lots of things by ourselves (and sometimes we do need a moment of solitude!) but it is usually not as fun or productive to do them alone. Satan uses this lie to make us believe independence equals strength. Here's how it often plays out:

1. **Self-Reliance Over God-Dependence**

   "You don't need God for this; you've got it under control." Satan tries to convince us to lean on our own understanding rather than trusting God's wisdom. You've got this! You're smart, driven, and experienced!

2. **Isolation From Community**

   "You don't need help from anyone. Asking for help is weakness." If I need someone else, then I feel like I am not enough. Like I am less valuable. I am the logjam in the river of progress instead of the multi-functioning excavator that can do it all. This lie leads to loneliness and cuts us off from the support God intended through relationships.

3. **Burnout and Frustration**

   When we try to carry life's burdens alone, we eventually reach our limits, leaving us overwhelmed, discouraged, and questioning our worth. *"Why do I always fail? Why can't I accomplish what I want to get done each day? Why don't I seem to be as capable as others?"*

"You Can Do This On Your Own"

The Truth About Our Need for God and Others

The Bible makes it clear we are not designed to go through life alone. One or two days of solitude by myself on a beach is great. One or two days alone in my house with my kids and I start to lose my mind. I want to take a special moment to recognize single moms, dads, and caregivers here. Anyone who is functioning as the sole provider for another human deserves all the recognition in the world. If this is you, please take some time for yourself and ask for help! Here's what God's Word teaches:

1. **We Are Created to Depend on God**

    Jesus said, "I am the vine; you are the branches. If you remain in me and I in you, you will bear much fruit; apart from me you can do nothing" (John 15:5). Wait. I must have read that wrong.

    What can you do apart from Christ?

    _____

    Can you make your heart beat or your lungs draw a breath? Not according to Job 33:4, "The Spirit of God has made me; the breath of the Almighty gives me life." Or Acts 17:25, which says, "And he is not served by human hands, as if he needed anything. Rather, he himself gives everyone life and breath and everything else."

    Wow, that really punches some holes in my theory about self-sufficiency. If I can't even breathe apart from God, how can I expect to do anything else? This explains all the times I tried to force something to happen (a guy to like me, my boss to promote me, the realtor to drop the price on a house) and not only did it not happen, it backfired. Miserably. The guy thought I was needy and emotionally unstable (true some days!), my boss demoted me (apparently being demanding is not a good quality in the service industry), and the realtor sold the house to someone who wasn't trying to be manipulative. I thought I was being strong and independent. Wrong. I was being prideful and ignorant. True strength and purpose come from abiding in Christ, not from our own efforts.

Write about a time you tried to make something happen on your own and it didn't work out:

_____
_____
_____
_____

What is something you are trying to do right now that you need to stop trying to do on your own and ask for help from God and others?

_____
_____
_____
_____

2. **We Are Called to Community**
   "Carry each other's burdens, and in this way you will fulfill the law of Christ" (Galatians 6:2). How does carrying each other's burdens fulfill the law of Christ?

"You Can Do This On Your Own"

Read Matthew 22:36-40. On what do the Law and Prophets (the law of Christ) hang?

_____

_____

So if we need to love God and others, what is one of the best ways we can do that? How do we show love? Through our actions. By helping them pack up and unpack when they move. By watching their kids so they can get a break. By sending them a letter or a text of encouragement. By taking them a meal when they are sick. Each of these is a way to help carry someone's burden.

God designed us to share life with others. Community provides encouragement, accountability, and mutual support. Not to mention, when I ask someone to help me carry my burden, sometimes they are able to find a way to solve the problem and get rid of the burden altogether. You never know if you never ask for help!

Who is someone with a burden you can help carry right now?

_____

Who is someone you can ask to help carry a burden you may have?

_____

_____

3. **God's Strength Is Made Perfect in Our Weakness**
   "But He said to me, 'My grace is sufficient for you, for my power is made perfect in weakness'" (2 Corinthians 12:9).

   Are we weak or strong according to this verse?
   _____
   _____

   This is not what I like to think. I like to think I'm strong. The truth is acknowledging our weakness and our need for God opens the door for His grace to work powerfully in our lives. Laura power is not enough to get me through the day. The days where I start by admitting that I need God's grace and power are the days I am able to live more victoriously.

How to Overcome This Lie

1. **Recognize Your Need for God**

   Pray daily for guidance, strength, and wisdom. Acknowledge that apart from Him, you can do nothing (John 15:5). Literally. You can't make your heart beat, your lungs fill with air, or the synapses in your brain fire. That is God, and you can't get out of bed in the morning without His strength. Surrender your plans to Him and trust in His provision.

2. **Cultivate Humility**

   Pride often keeps us trapped in self-reliance. Remember that humility isn't weakness. It's recognizing our dependence on God and His wisdom. Self-reliance is one of my biggest areas of opportunity because pride is my

"You Can Do This On Your Own"

biggest problem. Start with humility. Here are some ways to recognize what pride says and counter it with God's truth:

What Pride Says vs. What God Says

> **Pride Says:** "I deserve recognition and praise."
> **God Says:** "Humble yourselves before the Lord, and He will lift you up" (James 4:10).
>
> **Pride Says:** "I'm better than others."
> **God Says:** "Do nothing out of selfish ambition or vain conceit. Rather, in humility value others above yourselves" (Philippians 2:3).
>
> **Pride Says:** "I know what's best for me."
> **God Says:** "Trust in the Lord with all your heart and lean not on your own understanding" (Proverbs 3:5).
>
> **Pride Says:** "I don't need forgiveness."
> **God Says:** "If we confess our sins, He is faithful and just and will forgive us our sins and purify us from all unrighteousness" (1 John 1:9).
>
> **Pride Says:** "I can make my own plans."
> **God Says:** "Many are the plans in a person's heart, but it is the Lord's purpose that prevails" (Proverbs 19:21).
>
> **Pride Says:** "It's all about me."
> **God Says:** "Whoever wants to be My disciple must deny themselves and take up their cross daily and follow Me" (Luke 9:23).

Pride Says: "I earned all I have."
God Says: "Remember the Lord your God, for it is He who gives you the ability to produce wealth" (Deuteronomy 8:18).

Pride Says: "Admitting I'm wrong makes me weak."
God Says: "My grace is sufficient for you, for My power is made perfect in weakness" (2 Corinthians 12:9).

Pride Says: "I don't need God."
God Says: "God opposes the proud but shows favor to the humble" (James 4:6).

3. **Embrace Community**

   Surround yourself with Christ-centered relationships. Share your burdens, seek wise counsel, and allow others to pour into your life. God often uses people to fulfill His purposes. Sometimes this comes in the form of physical support and help from people. I can attest that moving from one house to another is MUCH easier with a community to help. Other times this is emotional support when you need a word of encouragement or a nudge of exhortation.

4. **Rest in God's Grace**

   Instead of striving to handle everything yourself, lean on God's grace. His strength sustains us when we feel weak, and His power carries us when we feel inadequate. All my striving usually leaves me burnt out, overextended, and physically unwell. I have gotten headaches and the flu (among other things) because my body was too worn out to fight anything off.

5. **Remember Jesus' Example**

    Even Jesus, the Son of God, modeled dependence on the Father and partnership with others. He prayed often and shared His ministry with His disciples, showing us the beauty of reliance and collaboration. Jesus, the One who needed no one, intentionally surrounded himself with people and was in constant communication with His Father. When He was tempted by Satan in the wilderness, Jesus didn't try to be self-reliant and fight him off. He quoted God's words in the Scriptures. He relied on the power of God, even though He could have just snapped His fingers and defeated Satan.

Living in Freedom

The next time Satan whispers, *"You can do this on your own,"* counter the lie with truth:

"I can do all things through Christ who strengthens me" (Philippians 4:13).

God doesn't call us to self-reliance; He calls us to trust in Him and walk with others. Life's burdens become lighter, and our purpose becomes clearer when we rely on His strength and the support of the community He's given us. You were never meant to do this alone. Lean into God, embrace His people, and walk in the freedom of His design for your life.

··· Week 8 ···

The Lie: "Following God Is too Hard and not Worth It"

I'M SURE YOU have heard the phrase, "The juice isn't worth the squeeze." I take this phrase literally sometimes, like when I pass over a watermelon or a pineapple at the store because I know how much work is involved in cutting it. Would I rather have fresh pineapple or twenty minutes? I'll choose the twenty minutes nine times out of ten. My sister-in-law, Tiffany, loves to cut fruit, and picking out the best-tasting fruit at the store is her superpower. Whenever she is at a party, I know she will be there with fresh fruit, and I consider it to be such a treat!

There are a myriad of other things that fall into that category, but less literally. For example, my friend Sarah has always wanted to do her taxes the long-form way, yet she uses TurboTax every year because of the amount of work it would take to learn how to do long-form taxes. This is just one reason why Sarah and I are friends. I have never once considered learning how to do long-form taxes, nor would I if given the chance. I need people in my life who know a thing or two about finances. For me, the juice is not worth the squeeze.

I don't mean you should never learn a new skill set or invest brain power in trying to understand something complicated just because it takes time and effort. I simply mean you have to weigh the value of the time you would spend learning against the value of the new skill you would acquire.

That is what is at the heart of the lie of Satan: *"Following God is too hard and not worth it."* He wants you to believe your immediate pleasure is worth more than your relationship with Christ. What does it look like to follow God? The answer to that question is not simple, and yet, at the same time, it is. It looks like obeying the Lord and doing what He would do if He were here. Which is what? Loving God and loving people.

If following God looks like loving people, it is the most difficult directive of all time. Loving people is time-consuming, mentally and emotionally draining, and it requires sacrifice. Think for a moment of the times you have loved well or been loved well. For me, these were times when someone showed up for me in a way that cost them something.

It looks like a friend offering to help me with a party or a project when I know they have a ton on their plate already. It looks like my husband making dinner when my day has been rough. It looks like my family offering to watch my kids so I can go to my dentist appointment. It looks like all the people who have forgiven me when I have offended, ignored, or hurt them in some way.

So, what does it look like when I am not loving people and following God? When I believe the lie of Satan that following God is too hard? It looks like me prioritizing my time or my task list over people. A very practical example of this is when I send the kids to their rooms to punish them for misbehaving instead of taking the time to ask questions, understand the heart of the issue, and offer guidance and coaching on how to make it right and avoid it in the future. "Go to your room!" takes 1.6 seconds to say. The conversation that is needed to parent in a God-honoring way takes a minimum of 15 minutes. Choosing to follow God in my parenting is hard and time-consuming.

This scenario is not isolated to parenting. How often are you short with a co-worker, friend, or family member because of the time (and emotional energy) it would take to engage with them in a meaningful way? The Bible is full of examples of Jesus stopping to have lengthy conversations with people. If He did it, I should be doing it.

The hard truth is that loving people is not always met with the response I am looking for. When I take the time to parent the kids, they don't say, "Wow, thank you, mom. I appreciate you taking the time to help me learn and grow. That was showing love." Instead, they usually just run off after the conversation to keep playing. While I know in my heart I did the right thing, there is no immediate gratification in the form of a "thank you," so it can start to get old pretty quickly.

"Following God Is too Hard and not Worth It"

Because it can be hard to see the immediate effects of loving people and following God, Satan likes to whisper the lie in our ears, *"This isn't worth it. It's too hard. You're not making an impact."*

This lie is designed to discourage us, making us question our commitment to Christ and the goodness of God's plan. But Scripture reveals a deeper truth: while following God WILL involve challenges, it leads to incomparable joy, purpose, and eternal life. Maybe it doesn't feel like that today. Maybe you are having a tough time recalling the joys of following God. Friend, this is when Satan's lie has the most power over you.

The Power of the Lie

This lie works because it preys on our natural desire for comfort and ease. Here's how Satan distorts our perspective:

1. **Exaggerating the Difficulties**

    He whispers, *"Look how much you'll have to give up. No one notices the effort you are putting in. The sacrifices are too great."* He highlights the costs while hiding the blessings.

2. **Downplaying the Rewards**

    Satan minimizes the joy, peace, and eternal hope that come from following God. He makes it seem like obedience to Christ leads only to hardship. If we are focused on the difficulties, we will be blind to the hope only Jesus can provide. Satan likes to take our eyes off Jesus by keeping us focused on ourselves and our issues (which we all have!). He also likes to downplay the rewards we cannot see (like joy, peace, and hope) and make us feel like tangible rewards (like a big kitchen, new clothes, cars that drive themselves) are what we should be chasing.

3. **Appealing to Immediate Gratification**

   He tempts us to focus on temporary pleasures, saying, *"Why wait for future rewards when you can enjoy life now?"* Some of the rewards of following Jesus will never be realized until we get to heaven. To me, on a rough day, this seems like a long time to wait.

The Truth About Following God

God's Word exposes Satan's lie and reminds us of the abundant life we have in Christ:

1. **Following God Brings True Freedom**

   "Then you will know the truth, and the truth will set you free" (John 8:32). While Satan wants us to believe that God's ways are restrictive, the truth is that His commands bring freedom from sin and its consequences. While giving of ourselves to follow Christ and love others seems tiresome, the truth is that loving yourself more than others is what leads to true weariness and misery.

   Read John 8:34. What does sin do to us according to that verse?

   _____
   _____
   _____

   Read John 8:36. What does Jesus do for us according to that verse?

"Following God Is too Hard and not Worth It"

_____
_____
_____

That stretch of verses (John 8:31-36) talks about how true freedom only comes from the truth we find in Jesus. Anything else is slavery, even if we don't recognize it immediately.

2. Obedience Leads to Blessing

"Blessed are all who fear the Lord, who walk in obedience to him" (Psalm 128:1).

God's path may not always be easy, but it is good. His commands lead to a life filled with peace, joy, purpose, and blessing. I'm not talking about physical blessings like wealth or power or position, but the blessings of healthy relationships with your friends and family and a clear conscience.

Do you feel like you are walking through a season where the blessings are hard to see?

_____
_____

What does your walk with the Lord look like right now?

_____
_____
_____

Are you doing your best to obey Him in all things?

_____
_____
_____

Are you loving others well?

_____
_____

If your honest answers to these questions are not great, it may be a sign you are believing the lie, "following God is too hard and not worth it."

3. **God Provides Strength for the Journey**

"I can do all things through Christ who strengthens me" (Philippians 4:13). No matter how your walk with Christ is going at the moment, there is hope! You are not walking alone! Following God isn't something we do in our own power. He doesn't stare down on us from heaven, sighing and rolling His eyes when we get it wrong or giving us a gold star on a chart when we get it right. He is with us. He is with us when we get it right. He is with us when we get it wrong. He equips us with His strength and grace to persevere.

I have said it before and I'll say it again: Laura power is not enough. The times in my life where I have seen the most success are the times when I stopped trying to do it on my own and started praying for wisdom and strength from the Lord. When I was intentional about being still and knowing that He is God, things start to click.

What does that verse say we are able to do through Christ?

_____

_____

What are some things you are struggling to do right now, maybe because you are relying on your own skills, strength, position, money, or power to do them?

_____

_____

_____

_____

We already talked about how following God by loving Him and loving others is incredibly difficult. God doesn't expect perfection. He doesn't expect you to do it alone.

What is one practical way you can rely on the strength of God to follow Him today?

_____

_____

_____

_____

4. **The Rewards Are Eternal**

"For our light and momentary troubles are achieving for us an eternal glory that far outweighs them all" (2 Corinthians 4:17). The difficulties of following Christ pale in comparison to the eternal joy and glory we'll experience in His presence. I'll never forget walking into the kitchen of a very dear family member who lost her eighteen-year-old daughter in a car accident. There, on the windowsill was a notecard with this verse written out.

I got tears in my eyes as I thought about this sweet woman who had experienced the greatest pain a mother can experience (which I would not consider at all light or momentary) and was still choosing to believe in and live out the truth of the Bible.

In 2 Corinthians 12:1-7, Paul talks about being caught up in heaven, either physically or through a vision. I believe God gave Paul a glimpse of what heaven is like. That is why, even though Paul experienced being:

- Beaten (*2 Corinthians 11:25*)
- Whipped (*2 Corinthians 11:24*)
- Stoned (*Acts 14:19*)
- Imprisoned (*2 Corinthians 11:23, Acts 16:23-27, Acts 28:16-31, 2 Timothy 1:16-17*)
- Shipwrecked (*2 Corinthians 11:25, Acts 27:13-44*)
- Threatened (*2 Corinthians 11:26-27*)
- Sleepless (*2 Corinthians 11:27*)
- Hungry (*2 Corinthians 11:27*)
- Thirsty (*2 Corinthians 11:27*)
- Exposed (*2 Corinthians 11:27*)
- Opposed by false teachers (*Galatians 1:6-7, 2 Timothy 4:14-15*)

He still considered these things to be "light and momentary troubles." That is how unfathomable the joy of heaven is. Whenever following God seems to be too hard or not worth it, stop thinking about what you're going through right now and turn your thoughts to what awaits you in heaven.

Read Revelation chapters 21 and 22. List some of the joys we can look forward to experiencing in heaven!

_____
_____
_____
_____
_____

How to Overcome This Lie

1. **Focus on God's Promises**

    Memorize and meditate on Scriptures that remind you of God's faithfulness, strength, and the eternal rewards of following Him. I cannot tell you how many times I've been trapped by a lie of Satan and I'm not even aware of it until I read a Bible verse that reminds me of the truth. Here are some references to get you started:

    Promises of God's Presence
    - God is always with us (Hebrews 13:5)
    - God is near to the brokenhearted (Psalm 34:18)

    Promises of Strength and Help
    - God will strengthen and uphold us (Isaiah 41:10)
    - God's grace is sufficient (2 Corinthians 12:9)

Promises of Forgiveness
- God forgives our sins (1 John 1:9)
- God removes our sins completely (Psalm 103:12)

Promises of Provision
- God will supply our needs (Philippians 4:19)
- God cares for us (1 Peter 5:7)

Promises of Peace
- God gives peace beyond understanding (Philippians 4:7)
- Jesus gives perfect peace (John 14:27)

Promises of Eternal Life
- Eternal life through Christ (John 3:16)
- No separation from God's love (Romans 8:38-39)

Promises of Guidance
- God directs our steps (Psalm 37:23)
- God's Word is a light for us (Psalm 119:105)

Promises of Victory
- God gives us victory in Christ (1 Corinthians 15:57)
- We are more than conquerors (Romans 8:37)

2. **Seek God's Presence Daily**

   Spend time in prayer and worship to draw close to God. His presence will renew your strength and remind you why He's worth following. There is a Latin phrase that I love, *Coram Deo*, which translates, "In the presence of God."[7] When I am intentional about talking to God throughout the day, I find I am better equipped to not only fight the lies of Satan but to be a better human. I also find that I can much more easily hear Him whispering back to me through the truths of Scripture.

Read Psalm 16:11. What does this verse say we can find in the presence of God?

_____

3. **Stay Connected to Community**

   Surround yourself with fellow believers who can encourage you, share their testimonies, and walk with you in faith. Friends, I absolutely need this. I need the people who can listen to me and then put me in my place. They can hear my complaining spirit or my lack of perspective or my pride before I even realize it's there, and then call it out. Rather than feeling attacked, I feel like light has just been shed on the issue, allowing me to see it and defeat it.

   Read 1 Thessalonians 5:11, Hebrews 3:13, Hebrews 10:24-25, and Colossians 3:16. What are some of the ways that being in community with our fellow believers can help us according to these verses?

   _____

   _____

   _____

   _____

4. **Remember Christ's Example**

   Jesus endured the ultimate sacrifice for our salvation. His life shows that the hard path is worth it when it leads to God's glory and our redemption. If anyone could say following God was too hard and not worth it, it would have been Jesus. Difficult does not even begin to describe His life and death. Yet He knew that it was worth it. He could see the end from the beginning. Even though I can't, I have to trust the truth of Scripture about the hope of heaven and an eternity with my Lord.

Read Mark chapter 15. What are some of the agonies Jesus suffered because of His love for the Father and for us?

_____

_____

_____

_____

Read Hebrews 12:2. What does this verse say that Jesus was focused on during that time of agony?

_____

_____

5. **Keep an Eternal Perspective**

   Life on earth is temporary, but eternity with God is forever. Fix your eyes on the bigger picture, trusting that the journey with Him is always worth it. Even though I can't spend time with the Lord face-to-face now, sometimes it feels like I can feel His face in the warm rays of the sun when I'm at the beach or in the eyes of someone special who says, "I love you" or in the soft fur of my rabbit when he cuddles up to me. It also seems like I can feel Him holding my hand when I'm sobbing over a loss, or a fight, or a feeling of despair. I think God gives us moments of His presence here on earth that make us anticipate living constantly in His presence in heaven.

Read James 1:12, Matthew 5:12, Matthew 25:21, 1 Corinthians 2:9. What are some of the things we have to look forward to in heaven according to these verses?

_____
_____
_____
_____
_____
_____

Living in Freedom

The next time Satan whispers, *"Following God is too hard and not worth it,"* respond with truth:

"I have decided to follow Jesus. No turning back!"

God never promised that the journey would be easy, but He promised it would be worth it. The peace, joy, and purpose you experience in Him far outweigh any temporary sacrifices. And the ultimate reward—eternal life with Him—is beyond what we can imagine.

Trust Him. Follow Him. And know that every step you take in obedience is leading you closer to His heart and His glory.

··· Week 9 ···

The Lie: "You Need _____ to Have Peace"

WHEN DO YOU feel peaceful? I feel the most peaceful when the house is clean, the bills are paid, the animals and kids are happy and healthy, I am caught up on assignments at work, and Tyler and I are cuddled up on the couch eating cheese and watching a movie.

The sad truth is that all of those things have not happened simultaneously in…ever. The house is never completely clean (dang those dusty baseboards!). Bills always seem to come due sooner than I would like. Between the sixty-five animals and three kids, something always needs to be fed or cleaned. I will never be caught up on work assignments, as part of my job is to think ahead and plan for the communication going

"You Need _____ to Have Peace"

out in the future. However, Tyler and I do cuddle up on the couch just about every night to eat snacks and watch a movie together (priorities, friends!).

The problem comes when many of those things are out of whack all at once. The house is a mess because I haven't found the time to clean since I've been overly busy with work assignments. One of the pets isn't eating well, one of the kids has a broken arm, and another one has pink eye. There is an unforeseen expense like the medical bill for the broken arm or the tire that blew out on the car, and now money is tight (financial planning is not my strength). I know many of you can likely relate, and have incredible stories of going through seasons where everything seemed to be crumbling around you.

In the hustle and chaos of life, peace can often feel elusive, and for good reason. Here are some parts of the Merriam-Webster Dictionary definition of peace: "A state of tranquility or quiet; freedom from disquieting or oppressive thoughts or emotions; harmony in personal relations."[8] The full definition is much longer.

Apparently we need a lot of things to come together in just the right way in order to experience peace. Even if our external circumstances are under control, we can still be plagued by our own thoughts and emotions. We long for calm amidst the noise, assurance in uncertainty, and rest for our weary souls. But there's a common lie Satan whispers to our hearts: *"You need _____ to find peace."*

He fills in the blank with countless counterfeits: success, money, approval, perfection, relationships, or possessions. He tells us constantly that if we could just work a little harder, buy a few more things, be a better person, lose weight, have a few more friends, then we could have peace. We could be happy. At least once a day I find myself thinking along these lines and have to take those thoughts captive before I allow myself to believe the lie Satan is constantly telling me. His false promises lure us with the idea that peace is just one achievement, one purchase, or one person away. Yet, when we chase these things, peace always seems to remain just out of reach.

What are some of the things you have tried to put in the blank space in an attempt to find peace?

_____
_____
_____
_____

The Root of the Lie

Here is the problem with the lie "You need _____ to find peace": We do need something outside of ourselves in order to find peace. Left to ourselves, peace is the last thing we will find. That is why so many are searching in so many places to find it. It is also why, even though I know the truth, I still fall prey to these thoughts too often. It is why stress and anxiety levels are at an all-time high.

According to the World Health Organization, an estimated four percent of the global population experiences an anxiety disorder, equating to approximately 301 million people.[9] The National Institute of Mental Health states that in the U.S., 19.1 percent of adults had any anxiety disorder in the past year.[10] Singlecare says that as of August 2024, 31 percent of adults surveyed globally considered stress the biggest health problem in their country.[11] According to the Mental Health Foundation, 51 percent of adults who felt stressed reported feeling depressed, and 61 percent reported feeling anxious.[12]

It's not that people are not searching for peace. They are. I know because sometimes I still find myself in the midst of chaos and praying for peace. The problem people have is they are searching in the wrong places. There are many things and people Satan wants us to think can fill in the blank and bring us peace. It's all a lie.

At its core, this deception diverts our focus from God, persuading us to believe that something other than Him can satisfy the deepest longings of our hearts. It's the same strategy Satan used in the garden with Eve—planting doubt in God's sufficiency and enticing her to seek fulfillment elsewhere. It deludes us into thinking, "You need God AND _____ to find peace."

But no amount of striving or acquiring can truly quiet the storm within. Money can't buy healthy relationships. Power can't quiet the anxious thoughts in our heads. You name it, it cannot bring you peace. That's because the peace we seek cannot be manufactured by the world. It is a gift only God can give. The truth is there is only one word that can fill in that blank and truly bring us peace. It is a name: Jesus.

The Truth About Peace

Jesus spoke directly to this in John 14:27: "Peace I leave with you; my peace I give to you. I do not give to you as the world gives. Do not let your hearts be troubled and do not be afraid." I so appreciate that Jesus points out that He gives differently than the world. The world often emphasizes giving that is conditional, limited, and often driven by expectations or self-interest. In contrast, God's giving is characterized by generosity, abundance, and unconditional love.

How the World Gives:

1. **Conditional Giving:** People often give based on expectations of receiving something in return—whether praise, acknowledgment, or material rewards. Can I get a "thank you" over here?
2. **Limited Resources:** Giving can be viewed as a finite resource, meaning people may hold back out of fear of running out. Have you ever had someone wealthy give you a "small" gift? Or someone gives you something even though they are in need themselves?

One of my favorite moments with my daughter, Tessa, was at Christmas time when I was helping her pick out gifts for her brothers. Tristan really wanted an action figure from one of his favorite cartoons. The problem is the cartoon is twenty years old, and they don't sell those action figures in stores anymore. This forced me to go to individual sellers on eBay, where the action figures are pricey because they are "collectibles." The one that Tristan really wanted was ridiculously priced, and I refused to pay that much for a two-inch piece of plastic. He was not going to get what he really wanted for Christmas, and Tessa knew it.

She told me that she wanted to use her own money to buy the action figure for Tristan. I tried to discourage her from doing it, citing the principle of paying more for something than what it is worth, but to Tessa, it was worth it. I told her it would cost her every penny she had saved up, and she immediately went and gave me her whole piggy bank. With a big smile on her face, she said, "I just can't wait to see the smile on Tristan's face when he opens this on Christmas morning!"

She gave everything she had to show love to her brother and make him feel special. I thought about all the gifts I had purchased for people and realized that I hadn't gotten anything nearly as special for anyone as Tessa had. She was giving like Jesus.

3. **Self-centered:** The focus is often on personal gain or recognition, leading to acts of giving that are transactional.
4. **Fear-Based:** Giving may be motivated by scarcity, control, or a desire to maintain power or security.

How God Gives:

1. **Abundant and Unconditional:** God's giving is characterized by limitless love and grace, offering forgiveness, peace, and provision without conditions. Thank goodness, because I could never do anything good enough or be good enough to earn those things.
2. **Overflowing Resources:** God's blessings are not limited by human constraints—His generosity is infinite.
3. **Selfless:** God gives without expecting anything in return, driven by compassion and mercy. I still have trouble comprehending how God can look on me with compassion and mercy instead of with disgust and disappointment. While I don't understand it, I am eternally grateful for it!

4. **Grace-Based:** God's giving flows from a place of trust, not fear, inviting people to receive freely.

This is how God gives us peace. True peace isn't dependent on external circumstances or material gains. It is rooted in the unchanging nature of God and His promises. When we rest in His love, trust His plan, and surrender to His will, we experience a peace that surpasses understanding. "And the peace of God, which transcends all understanding, will guard your hearts and your minds in Christ Jesus" (Philippians 4:7).

This is what makes it possible for two of my friends in their thirties, one with four young children, and one of my cousins in her forties with three kids, to receive a diagnosis of aggressive cancer and constantly talk about their joy, hope, and peace. These women and many others like them are superheroes. Not because they have found a way to make everything go right but because they are refusing to believe Satan's lie that they need health to have peace.

They are the ones I think of when I start to get anxious about finances or my dirty house. My late electric bill and dirty baseboards are nothing compared to their chemo and radiation treatments. And guess what? No diagnosis, job lay-off, or emotional hurt is bigger than God. I love the quote from Dr. David Jeremiah, "Don't tell God how big your problems are, tell your problems how big your God is."

How to Overcome the Lie

1. **Identify the Blank**

    Ask yourself: What is Satan trying to convince me I need for peace? Is it success, approval, or control?

"You Need _____ to Have Peace"

Naming the lie is the first step to defeating it. It is okay if there are multiple items in the blank.

2. **Refocus on God's Promises**

   Fill your mind with Scripture that declares God's sufficiency. Remind yourself that He alone is the source of lasting peace. Meditate on verses like these:

   - Isaiah 26:3: "You will keep in perfect peace those whose minds are steadfast because they trust in you."

   What does "perfect peace" look like to you?

   _____

   _____

   _____

   Who does this verse say will be kept in "perfect peace?"

   _____

   _____

   _____

   How do we get minds that are steadfast?

   _____

   _____

   _____

   Trusting God rather than in ourselves leads to peace!

- 2 Peter 1:3: "His divine power has granted to us all things that pertain to life and godliness, through the knowledge of him who called us to his own glory and excellence" (ESV).

    What have we been granted through God's divine power?

    _____
    _____
    _____

    How does this verse reinforce that God is all we need?

    _____
    _____
    _____

- Matthew 6:33: "But seek first the kingdom of God and his righteousness, and all these things will be added to you" (ESV).

    What two things does this verse say we should be seeking?

    _____
    _____
    _____

    What does seeking first the kingdom of God and His righteousness look like for you?

    _____
    _____
    _____

"You Need _____ to Have Peace"

I once heard a speaker say, "If I'm taking care of God's business, He will take care of mine." I love that. The more we focus on God, the more we will be consumed by Him and the less headspace we have to be focused on our own weaknesses and struggles.

3. **Surrender the Struggle**

   Let go of the pursuit of things that were never meant to carry the weight of your peace. Lay your burdens at Jesus' feet and trust Him to meet your needs. Why is it that I still get disappointed when people and products don't live up to my expectations? It is unfair of me to think they could ever bring me lasting peace in the first place.

   Is there something or someone you were counting on that let you down? Take this moment to forgive them and commit to only expecting Jesus to meet your needs.

4. **Cultivate Gratitude**

   Gratitude shifts our perspective from lack to abundance. When we focus on God's blessings, we become less susceptible to the lie that we need "more" to be at peace. Here are some verses to help!

   - **1 Thessalonians 5:18**

     "Give thanks in all circumstances; for this is the will of God in Christ Jesus for you" (ESV).

   - **Colossians 3:17**

     "And whatever you do, in word or deed, do everything in the name of the Lord Jesus, giving thanks to God the Father through him" (ESV).

- **Psalm 100:4**

  "Enter his gates with thanksgiving and his courts with praise; give thanks to him and praise his name."

- **Ephesians 5:20**

  "Giving thanks always and for everything to God the Father in the name of our Lord Jesus Christ" (ESV).

- **Philippians 4:6**

  "Do not be anxious about anything, but in everything by prayer and supplication with thanksgiving let your requests be made known to God" (ESV).

- **Psalm 34:1**

  "I will bless the Lord at all times; his praise shall continually be in my mouth" (ESV).

Make a list of some of the things you can thank God for right now!

_____
_____
_____
_____

5. **Pray for Renewal**

   Ask the Holy Spirit to renew your mind and remind you of your identity in Christ. Prayer is a powerful tool for reclaiming peace in moments of doubt and struggle.

"You Need _____ to Have Peace"

A Life of True Peace

Peace isn't found in filling the blank with the world's offerings. It's found in Jesus, who fills every void and satisfies every longing. The next time the enemy whispers, *"You need _____ to find peace,"* reject the lie and declare this truth:

"The Lord is my shepherd; I lack nothing" (Psalm 23:1).

When we embrace this truth, we step into a peace that no circumstance, lie, or temptation can take away.

··· Week 10 ···

The Lie: "You'll Never Change"

THERE'S NOTHING QUITE as defeating as repeated failure. When I was eleven, I spent at least eight hours trying to get past a certain level in the Donkey Kong video game. I think there were mine carts involved. You would think after the first few tries, I would have moved on to a different activity or a different game, but nope. I kept playing. I kept failing. Eventually I got so discouraged I threw the controller against the wall. It broke. It was my friend's controller. Way to go, Laura. Sorry, Sarah!

I remember losing tennis games repeatedly and feeling similarly frustrated, although I didn't throw the racquet. I remember multiple batches of cookies that tasted gross or were burned. I'm sure I threw the remaining dough at something. I remember trying to get a boy to like me in middle

"You'll Never Change"

school. During those awkward years I was probably doomed before I started. Fail. Then there was my biggest repeat failure I discussed at length in the introduction: failing to tell the truth.

Repeated failure in that area was my most costly defeat. I can remember even in moments where I desperately wanted to change, to stop lying, hearing Satan whisper this lie to me: "You'll never change." I started to believe it. I had failed so many times. Why would trying again be any different? Why even bother trying at all? I will just get the same results. We all know the definition of insanity attributed to Albert Einstein (although likely not his quote): "Doing the same thing over and over and expecting different results."

If I don't feel like changing, what are my options? Give up? Unfortunately, that is what happens too much of the time. What does that look like? It looks like living in a rut. It looks like going through your day on autopilot. Doing the same things and not really finding meaning in them.

If this is you, I can tell you what you will do next week. You will talk to mostly the same people, eat mostly the same food, and engage in mostly the same activities. For those of you old enough to remember it, this reminds me of the cartoon series "The Pinky and the Brain." The show featured two lab rats who tried to take over the world every night.

I loved the banter between the incredibly smart mouse and the mouse who acted like he had no brain at all. Their schemes would never work, and things would always end in some goofy catastrophe. At the end of each episode, Brain would turn to Pinky and say, "We must prepare for tomorrow night." Pinky would then ask, "Why, what are we going to do tomorrow night, Brain?" To which Brain would reply, "The same thing we do every night, Pinky. Try to take over the world!" While the specifics of each episode are different, every single one follows the same basic plot.

Does this sound familiar? Do you find yourself stuck in a rut with your relationships, your job, your schedule, your sins? *"You'll never change."* It's a lie that echoes in the darkest moments, whispered to discourage and defeat us. Satan uses it to make us believe that our struggles are permanent, our efforts are futile, and our identity is tied to our past mistakes.

This is because change takes effort and can feel impossible at times. But here's the truth: Change is not only possible—it's promised when we place our faith in Jesus Christ. At the moment of salvation, if you have given your life to Christ, the most momentous change of your life takes place. You go from being a slave to sin, an enemy of God, destined for death and hell to being freed to new life in Christ, a son or daughter of God, who will spend all of eternity in heaven. The Bible talks about this transformation in 2 Corinthians 5:17: "Therefore, if anyone is in Christ, he is a new creation. The old has passed away; behold, the new has come" (ESV).

Great, you say. I remember when I accepted Christ and felt like a new creation, but that was years ago. I don't feel so new anymore. Now I feel like I can't live up to all the commands and standards of the Bible. I feel like sin defeats me every day. I feel like there are parts of me that I can't change.

Oh friend, I was there. For years. I was in anguish. "I asked Jesus into my heart," I thought, "Why don't I feel joyful? Why can't I stop lying? What's wrong with me?"

While I can't speak to your specific situation, I can tell you what my problem was: I gave my heart to Jesus, but I kept parts of my life to myself. I was still trying to drive the bus. I thought there were still some things I could do on my own as we talked about in week seven. Although I accepted that my salvation was accomplished by God, I took ownership of all subsequent growth and change.

Now it sounds delusional. I did nothing to earn or deserve or bring about my salvation, why would my sanctification be any different? It isn't. God is still the one doing all the work. All He asks of me is to surrender to that work. To stop trying to control my life. To stop trying to do His job. I can't do it. That's when I feel like a failure who will never change.

The Root of the Lie

Satan thrives on keeping us stuck. If he can convince us that transformation is impossible, we're more likely to give up, settle for less, or repeat destructive patterns. The enemy's goal is to isolate us from the truth of God's Word, where hope, renewal, and redemption abound.

Satan also likes us to think that the burden to change is all on us. If that were the case, true change would be impossible. Thank the Lord that He is constantly at work in us to sanctify us and make us more like Him. On my own, I would lose the battle every time.

This lie feeds on shame and guilt, reminding us of every failure and whispering, *"This is just who you are. You'll never be free from this."* But those are not God's words. His voice speaks life, growth, and restoration. I once heard a sermon where the pastor said, "I am so grateful that God will make all things new rather than making all new things."

Rather than give up on someone like me, who has spent seasons stuck in sin and start over with someone else, the Lord continues to faithfully, patiently work on my heart to take off the old and put on the new.

The Truth About Change

God is in the business of transformation. When we surrender our lives to Him, He begins a work in us that He will carry to completion. As the Bible says in Philippians 1:6, "Being confident of this, that he who began a good work in you will carry it on to completion until the day of Christ Jesus." Through the power of the Holy Spirit, we are continually being renewed, reshaped, and restored. This truth reminds us that change isn't solely about self-effort; it's about allowing God to work in and through us.

How to Overcome the Lie

1. **Reject the Lie and Replace It with Truth**

    When Satan says, "You'll never change," counter it with God's promises:

    - "I can do all things through Christ who strengthens me" (Philippians 4:13, NKJV).

        What is Paul referring to when he says "all things" in the context of Philippians 4? (Hint: Consider the verses before and after this one.)

"You'll Never Change"

_____

What does "all things" mean in the context of your life?

_____

Are there areas where you feel limited or empowered by this promise?

_____

How have you experienced Christ strengthening you in the past?

_____

Is there a current challenge where you need to rely more on Christ's strength?

_____
_____
_____

What does this verse teach you about the relationship between your efforts and Christ's empowerment?

_____
_____
_____

- "For with God, nothing will be impossible" (Luke 1:37, NKJV).

What was the context in which this statement was made?

_____
_____
_____

How does understanding the angel's message to Mary enhance your understanding of this verse?

_____
_____
_____

"You'll Never Change"

What does this verse teach about God's character and His ability to work in our lives?

_____
_____
_____

How does this truth challenge you to surrender control and depend on God's strength instead of your own?

_____
_____
_____

Speak these verses over your life, allowing the truth to silence the enemy's lies.

2. **Acknowledge the Process**

   Change doesn't happen overnight, and that's okay. Transformation is a journey of small, consistent steps in the right direction. Be patient with yourself as God works in your heart and life. Sometimes just being able to recognize your areas of opportunity and the need for change is a huge victory.

   Read Ephesians 4:10-13. Who does God give His people to help us?

   _____
   _____
   _____

How do these verses make reaching maturity sound like a process?

_____
_____
_____

3. **Rely on God's Strength, Not Your Own**

   True change comes from God, not from sheer willpower. Pray for His guidance and strength daily, trusting Him to do what you cannot.

   Read 1 Thessalonians 5:23-24. Who is the one doing the work of sanctification in these verses?

   _____
   _____

   Read 2 Peter 1:3-4. How do we get everything we need to live a godly life according to these verses?

   _____
   _____
   _____

4. **Surround Yourself with Support**

   God often uses community to encourage and strengthen us. Share your struggles with trusted friends, mentors, or a small group who will pray with you and hold you accountable.

5. Celebrate Progress

Recognize and celebrate the small victories along the way. Each step of obedience, no matter how small, is evidence of God's work in you. Every time you choose to forgive rather than hold a grudge, be patient rather than lash out, put someone else's feelings or wants ahead of your own, you have won a victory.

What are some actions you have taken that you can count as victories?

_____
_____
_____
_____

6. Remember God's Faithfulness

Instead of looking at who you want to be and getting discouraged because you're not there yet, look at the person you used to be and reflect on how far you've already come with God's help. His past faithfulness is a reminder that He will continue to guide and transform you.

Fill out at least five items in each column:

Past you	Current you	Future you

A Life of Ongoing Transformation

When Satan says, *"You'll never change,"* remind him that God's power is greater than any stronghold, habit, or past mistake. You are not defined by your failures—you are defined by who you are in Christ.

"And we all, who with unveiled faces contemplate the Lord's glory, are being transformed into His image with ever-increasing glory, which comes from the Lord, who is the Spirit" (2 Corinthians 3:18).

Change is not only possible; it's part of God's plan for your life. Trust in His promises, lean into His grace, and rest in the assurance that He is making all things new—including you.

Closing Comments

For any of you who were wondering, my first marriage—the one riddled with cheating and lying on my part—ended in divorce. I learned the hard way the severe consequences even "small" lies can have. I implore you to learn from my story and take the spiritual battle with Satan and his lies seriously.

I genuinely thank you for joining me as we explored the truths of God's Word and how we can combat the lies of Satan. It's clear from Scripture that Satan is the father of lies (John 8:44), and his primary tactic is to deceive, discourage, and distort God's truth in our lives.

We've seen how Satan tries to attack our identity, our confidence, and our relationship with God. However, God's Word equips us with the truth, reminding us we are loved, forgiven, and victorious in Christ. As we've discovered, the key to overcoming these lies is not relying on our own strength but leaning into God's truth and His promises.

- 1 Peter 5:8-9 reminds us to be vigilant and stand firm in our faith, knowing that God is greater than any lie.
- Ephesians 6:10-18 teaches us to put on the full armor of God, which includes His truth, righteousness, and

the Word of God, to protect ourselves from the enemy's schemes.

As we go forward, may we cling to God's truth and recognize the lies of Satan when they come.

Let's renew our minds daily with His Word, stand firm in faith, and remember that nothing can separate us from the love of God (Romans 8:38-39).

Let's pray God gives us the strength and discernment to walk in His truth and overcome every lie of the enemy.

Let's remember that "The one who is in you is greater than the one who is in the world" (1 John 4:4).

Let's compete with deceit. God bless you!

Endnotes

1. "What Are the Gates of Hell Jesus Talked About?" Maddy Rager. *BibleStudyTools*, 2023. Accessed 12 February 2025. https://www.biblestudytools.com/bible-study/topical-studies/what-are-gates-of-hell-jesus-talked-about.html

2. "Hymn: Jesus Loves the Little Children," hymnalnet RSS, accessed March 6, 2025, https://www.hymnal.net/en/hymn/c/58.

3. "Stress: statistics." *Mental Health Foundation*, 2025. https://www.mentalhealth.org.uk/explore-mental-health/statistics/stress-statistics. Accessed 7 Feb. 2025.

4. Saint Louis University. "Link between adversity, psychiatric and cognitive decline." *ScienceDaily*. www.sciencedaily.com/releases/2024/03/240301134756.htm. Accessed 7 Feb. 2025.

5. Xiang X. et al. "Childhood adversity and cognitive impairment in later life." *Frontiers in Psychology*, 2022. 10.3389/fpsyg.2022.935254. Accessed 7 Feb. 2025.

6. Merriam-Webster.com Dictionary, s.v. "righteous," accessed February 11, 2025, https://www.merriam-webster.com/dictionary/righteous.

7. "In the Presence of God." Ron Jones. *Something Good with Ron Jones*, 2018. https://www.somethinggoodradio.org/blog/in-the-presence-of-god. Accessed February 12, 2025.

8   Merriam-Webster.com Dictionary, s.v. "peace," accessed February 11, 2025, https://www.merriam-webster.com/dictionary/peace.

9   "Anxiety disorders." *World Health Organization.* 2023. https://www.who.int/news-room/fact-sheets/detail/anxiety-disorders. Accessed February 12, 2025.

10   "Any Anxiety Disorder." *National Institute of Mental Health.* https://www.nimh.nih.gov/health/statistics/any-anxiety-disorder. Accessed February 12, 2025.

11   "Stress statistics 2024: How common is stress, and who's most affected?" *Singlecare.* 2024. https://www.singlecare.com/blog/news/stress-statistics. Accessed February 12, 2025.

12   "Stress: statistics." *Mental Health Foundation, 2025.* https://www.mentalhealth.org.uk/explore-mental-health/statistics/stress-statistics. Accessed 7 Feb. 2025.

About the Author

Laura Worosher holds a Bachelor of Science in Communications from Cedarville University and spent ten years in customer service and retail. After marrying and welcoming her first child, she chose to become a stay-at-home mom. A few years later, she transitioned to working from home as a web content writer.

A divine encounter outside her church sparked the beginning of her career in business as an executive assistant. This opportunity paved the way for Laura to start a business, Beacon Insights, which aims to be a platform and community offering hope and inspiration through books, seminars, and training materials.

Currently, Laura homeschools her three children, serves as the President of Beacon Insights, actively contributes to two other businesses, and manages a private petting zoo with over sixty animals.

She is also the author of the best-selling book *Blind to Hope*, about how the Lord saved both Laura and the biblical character Bartimaeus from different types of blindness and is ready to save you, too.

Connect with Laura at BeaconInsights.net.

www.ingramcontent.com/pod-product-compliance
Lightning Source LLC
Chambersburg PA
CBHW050224100526
44585CB00017BA/1969